FLOODED WITH LIGHT

A 53-Week Devotional

Published by **3 Point Turn Publishing**
Brea, CA

ISBN: 979-8-9941140-1-8

First Edition

Printed in the United States of America

FLOODED WITH LIGHT

Biblical revelations to equip the believer

to walk in the supernatural

Joshua & Mireya Tufano

Table of Contents

INTRODUCTION VII

SECTION 1: FOUNDATIONS OF FAITH, WEEKS 1-12

WEEK 1: THE BAPTISM OF THE HOLY SPIRIT 1
WEEK 2: BELIEVE AND RECEIVE 7
WEEK 3: BUT GOD 13
WEEK 4: PAID IN FULL: NOTING MISSING, NOTHING BROKEN 17
WEEK 5: THE BLOOD! 23
WEEK 6: THE BRIDGE 27
WEEK 7: THE DEBT HAS BEEN PAID 31
WEEK 8: SPIRIT, SOUL, AND BODY 37
WEEK 9: KNOWLEDGE>FEELINGS 41
WEEK 10: YOU ARE NOT YOUR FLESH: PART 1 45
WEEK 11: YOU ARE NOT YOUR FLESH: PART 2 51
WEEK 12: YOU ARE NOT YOUR FLESH: PART 3 57

SECTION 2: GROWTH & TRANSFORMATION, WEEKS 13-21

WEEK 13: INSIDE OUT: NOT THE MOVIE 65
WEEK 14: GUARD YOUR HEART: SAFEGUARDING YOUR INNOCENCE
.... 69
WEEK 15: HEALING IS IN YOUR SPIRIT: FOR YOUR BODY 75
WEEK 16: HEALING IS IN YOUR SPIRIT: FOR YOUR HEART 81
WEEK 17: HEALING THE HEART: THE PURPOSE OF FAITH 87
WEEK 18: CALLED OUT 93
WEEK 19: MATURING IN CHRIST 97
WEEK 20: BLANK CANVAS 103
WEEK 21: RELY ON JESUS 107

SECTION 3: THE ROMANS 5 PROCESS, WEEKS 22-25

WEEK 22: PART 1: PERSEVERANCE 115
WEEK 23: PART 2: CHARACTER 121
WEEK 24: PART 3.1: HOPE 127
WEEK 25: PART 3.2: HOPE 133

SECTION 4: IDENTITY & AUTHORITY IN CHRIST, WEEKS 26-31

WEEK 26: AMBASSADORS OF HEAVEN 141
WEEK 27: HEAVEN BACKS YOU UP: YOU HAVE THE AUTHORITY 147
WEEK 28: THE POWER OF SONSHIP 153

Week 29: The Power of Attentive Ears 159
Week 30: The Power of Gratitude 163
Week 31: The Power of Love 169

SECTION 5: GUARDING AGAINST SPIRITUAL PITFALLS, WEEKS 32-39

Week 32: Pride 177
Week 33: Stubborn Unbelief 181
Week 34: Victory Over Familiarity 185
Week 35: When Religion Hates Your Rising 191
Week 36: Victory & Defeat 197
Week 37: No Better, But Worse 201
Week 38: No Law=No Punishment 207
Week 39: Freedom From Curses 211

SECTION 6: FEAR, FOCUS & PERSPECTIVE, WEEKS 40-43

Week 40: Fear: Not the Holy Kind 219
Week 41: Fearing God Over Man 225
Week 42: Where is Your Focus 231
Week 43: Where is Your Treasure? 237

SECTION 7: LIVING FROM HEAVEN'S REALITY, WEEKS 44-53

Week 44: Compassion 245
Week 45: God is Willing and Able 249
Week 46: Greater Glory 253
Week 47: The Holy Cover Up 257
Week 48: The Pivot into Higher Levels of Strength 261
Week 49: The Recipe for Peace 267
Week 50: Mysteries Revealed 271
Week 51: Faith Turns Weakness into Strength 275
Week 52: Give Credit Where Credit is Due 279
Week 53: The Power of the Seed: Be a Sower! 283

Introduction

We are overjoyed that you have received this devotional, and we truly believe it will be a blessing in your life. Before we begin, I want to share the heart behind its title, Flooded With Light.

Ephesians 1:18 NLT *"I pray that your hearts will be flooded with light so that you can understand the confident hope He has given to those He called—His holy people who are His rich and glorious inheritance."*

In this verse, the apostle Paul describes a deeper knowing of God that comes by revelation. Other translations phrase it as "the eyes of your understanding" being "flooded with light." Throughout Scripture, light often symbolizes revelation, while spiritual blindness is portrayed as darkness.

Think about it: we see naturally when light enters our eyes, is transformed into signals, and then processed by our brain into the images we recognize. Light must first penetrate in order to be understood. Physical blindness, on the other hand, means that light cannot enter and therefore cannot be processed. The same principle applies spiritually. When the "eyes of our heart" are healthy, light is able to pass through and bring revelation. We begin to see what

God's Word says within us. But when spiritual blindness prevails, our eyes are unhealthy, and the light of revelation cannot enter.

2 Corinthians 4:3–4 *"But even if our gospel is veiled, it is veiled to those who are perishing, whose minds the god of this age has blinded, who do not believe, lest the light of the gospel of the glory of Christ, who is the image of God, should shine on them."*

With this book, our prayer is that as you meditate on the revelations within, insights the Lord has entrusted to us over the last 12 years, the eyes of your understanding would be opened and filled with His light. For when sight comes, there is clarity. In the same way, when spiritual sight comes, there is a deep inner knowing: I know I have what God's Word declares, because I can see it on the inside. Our prayer is that this revelation floods your heart and transforms your life.

This is a 53-week devotional designed to be read over the course of a year. Each entry includes additional tools to help you meditate on and apply the revelation:

- **Light for the Path** – the key takeaway from the week's devotion, summarized.
- **Deeper Light: Reflect + Respond** has several sections such as **Read More** – supplemental verses for meditation throughout the week.
- **Journal Prompt** – a guided reflection to help you interact with the Word personally.
- **Daily Declarations of Faith** – a Scripture-based declaration to speak over your life. As Proverbs 18:21 says, "Death and life are in the power of the tongue." Speaking God's Word, regardless of how you feel, is vital to seeing it manifest.
- **Live It Out** – a practical step of obedience to put your faith into action. For as James reminds us, "Faith without works is dead" (James 2:26).

Each of these sections has been prayerfully designed to take the revelation you receive and move it from head knowledge into the soil of your heart. From receiving the truth, to reflecting on your journey, to declaring God's promises, and finally putting them into practice; this devotional is meant to lead you into a depth with God you may never have experienced before. If you follow it faithfully, we believe this year will be one of the most expansive and transformative of your life.

Before we begin this journey, let's pray together:

Prayer

"Heavenly Father, I thank You for Your Word that brings life. Thank You that no matter what I face, if I cling to Your Word and hold fast to my confession of faith, I will see Your promises come to pass, for You are faithful and cannot lie. I choose to open my eyes to receive divine revelation. May the light of Your Word flood the eyes of my understanding, that I may know the hope of Your calling and all its glorious benefits. Let me not only know Your Word, but experience it—receiving healing, freedom, and transformation in every area of my life. I humble myself before You, Lord, and approach Your Word with openness and fresh expectation. Grant me this in greater measure, I pray, in Jesus' name. Amen."

Enjoy the journey ahead!

SECTION 1

FOUNDATIONS

of

FAITH

Weeks 1–12

The Baptism of the Holy Spirit: Empowered for the Supernatural

The Bible clearly describes two distinct experiences with the Holy Spirit that must take place in the life of a believer in order to walk in the fullness of God's gift that He provided through the death and resurrection of Jesus Christ.

One of these experiences is mentioned in:

John 20:22 – *"And when He had said this, He breathed on them, and said to them, 'Receive the Holy Spirit.'"*

Here, Jesus breathed on His disciples, and they received the Holy Spirit. This moment marks the first conversion of fallen humanity into the family of God. It was the moment the Holy Spirit came to dwell within them, sealing them until the day when the rest of their being, body and soul, would be redeemed (see **Ephesians 1:13–14**).

After this, Scripture says that Jesus was seen by them over a period of forty days, speaking to them about things concerning the Kingdom of God (see **Acts 1:3**). At the end of that period, just before His ascension, Jesus gave them this command:

Acts 1:4–5, 8 *"And being assembled together with them, He commanded them not to depart from Jerusalem, but to wait for the Promise of the Father, 'which,' He said, 'you have heard from Me; for John truly baptized with water, but you shall be baptized with the Holy Spirit not many days from now… But you shall receive power when the Holy Spirit has come upon you; and you shall be witnesses to Me in Jerusalem, and in all Judea and Samaria, and to the end of the earth.'"*

The Promise of the Father, spoken through the prophets, involved not only the Holy Spirit dwelling within us, but also coming upon us for power (see **Ezekiel 36:26–27, Joel 2:28–29**). When the Holy Spirit comes upon a person, there is always supernatural evidence. Therefore, in **Acts 1,** Jesus wasn't speaking of salvation; they had already received the Holy Spirit that abides within in John 20. He was now speaking of an empowerment for service.

Jesus said:

John 14:12 *"Whoever believes in Me will also do the works that I do; and greater works than these will he do…"*

The power of the Holy Spirit coming upon someone is what empowers them to fulfill these works. Miracles cannot be performed by human effort, they require supernatural power! That power is made available through the baptism of the Holy Spirit.

Can someone be saved and yet not baptized in the Holy Spirit? Yes, it is possible, but it is not God's desire. A believer who has not received the baptism of the Spirit lives a life castrated of power. Consider this example:

Acts 19:1–7 *"And it happened, while Apollos was at Corinth, that Paul, having passed through the upper regions, came to Ephesus. And finding some disciples he said to them, "Did you receive the Holy Spirit when you believed?" So they said to him, "We have not so much as heard whether there is a Holy Spirit." And he said to them, "Into what then were you baptized?" So they said, "Into John's baptism." Then Paul said, "John indeed baptized with a baptism of repentance, saying to the people that they should believe on Him who would come after him, that is, on Christ Jesus." When they heard this, they were baptized in the name of the Lord Jesus. And when Paul had laid hands on them, the Holy Spirit came upon them, and they spoke with tongues and prophesied."*

Note that they were already disciples, already saved. However, Paul discerned that something was missing: the baptism into the power of the Holy Spirit. Once they received it, the supernatural followed.

Speaking in tongues and prophesying are not just emotional expressions. They are powerful tools that build up both the individual and the church. Moreover, they are made available only through the baptism of the Holy Spirit.

As followers of Jesus, the God-Man who rose from the dead, we are called into a supernatural life. After all, how many people have risen from the grave? Only One, Jesus! So why do we struggle to believe for the supernatural, when our very faith is built upon it?

Many have allowed the natural realm to define what is possible. We've created doctrines that explain away our lack of power, soothing our conscience instead of stirring our faith. But to live without power is to live in disobedience to Heaven's mandate (see **Mark 16:15–18**).

If you find yourself in that place, saved, but not baptized in the Holy Spirit, I invite you to receive it right now. You don't have to go another moment without the power God promised you.

The Holy Spirit will ignite you with passion and power to overthrow everything that once had dominion over you. You will walk in victory and boldness!

Everything with God is simple and that includes receiving the baptism of the Holy Spirit. Like salvation, it is received by faith:

Colossians 2:6 *"As you therefore have received Christ Jesus the Lord, so walk in Him…"*

You received salvation by faith, and you receive the baptism of the Holy Spirit the same way.

If you are ready to receive the Baptism of the Holy Spirit, pray this from your heart:

Prayer

"Father, I thank You for the gift of salvation and the empowerment of the Spirit. By faith, I now receive the baptism of the Holy Spirit, and through it, the power to become Your witness in whatever capacity You have destined for me. Thank You for it, and may the name of Jesus be lifted high in all the fruit that my life bears."

Congratulations! You've received the baptism of the Holy Spirit. Now begin to speak in tongues by faith. Let the Holy Spirit lead you. You may begin with just a few syllables or an entire flow. Yield to Him.

Make this part of your daily life, especially in worship, prayer, and time in the Word. As you do, you will grow in it. You were born again to live a Spirit-empowered life. Don't settle for anything less.

Light for the Path

The baptism of the Holy Spirit is God's appointed empowerment for every believer, releasing supernatural boldness and authority to fulfill His calling.

Deeper Light – Reflect + Respond

1. Read More

- Acts 2:1–4
- Luke 24:49
- Joel 2:28–29
- 1 Corinthians 14:1-4,13-15
- 2 Timothy 1:6–7

2. Journal Prompt

- Have I been walking in the supernatural power God intended for me, or have I been relying on my own strength?
- In what areas of my life do I need the Spirit's power to replace my own strength?
- What fears or misconceptions might be holding me back from fully receiving the baptism of the Holy Spirit?

3. Daily Declaration of Faith

"I am filled and empowered by the Holy Spirit. His power rests upon me, His fire flows through me, and I walk in the supernatural life God has called me to live."

4. Live It Out

- If you haven't yet, pray in faith, the prayer to receive the baptism of the Holy Spirit that is at the end of this devotion.
- Dedicate time each day to pray in the Spirit and worship God.
- Step out in boldness; pray for someone's healing, share the Gospel, or encourage someone with a Spirit-led word.

Reflection

_____

_____

_____

_____

_____

_____

_____

_____

_____

_____

_____

_____

_____

_____

_____

_____

_____

_____

Week 2

Believe and Receive

Mark 11:24 *"Therefore I say to you, whatever things you ask when you pray, believe that you receive them, and you will have them."*

There once was a king named Orelian, who reigned over the Kingdom of the Seven Waters, a realm founded upon one immutable law: every citizen could only receive according to their expectations. To impose one's will upon another without consent was deemed a violation of the highest order, a transgression likened to spiritual assault. This sacred law upheld the dignity of all within the kingdom, safeguarding their freedom to choose their own path. It was a land of true liberty, where each individual would ultimately give account for how they used that freedom for the good stored up in their hearts, or for evil.

The delight of King Orelian's heart, and the crowning jewel of his kingdom, were his two beloved sons; Janthar and Doombar. Equal in stature and rank, each bore their father's likeness in distinct and noble ways. The king loved them both without measure or favoritism, for such was the nature of this just and righteous ruler. His kingdom overflowed with blessing and life for all who renounced their former citizenship in the Outlands, a desolate realm ruled by the tyrant usurper, Lord Malgrith.

Yet many who entered the Kingdom of the Seven Waters failed to partake in its abundance. Though freed outwardly, their hearts remained tethered to their past allegiances. They projected the cruelty of their former master onto the compassionate King Orelian, unable to accept that his heart was wholly good. Tragically, this was true even of one of the king's own sons. Though raised in the royal court, his heart turned toward the Outlands. Its corrupting influence crept in subtly, distorting his perception of his father. Suspicion took root, convincing him that even the king's kindness was a mask for manipulation.

Each son was entrusted with rulership over distinct realms within the kingdom, serving as royal stewards under their father's authority. As part of their duties, they were to appear before the throne to request provisions necessary to fulfill their charge and uphold the kingdom's law. What follows is an account of one such instance.

The second-born, Prince Janthar, came first. He needed materials to rebuild towns ravaged by Outland attacks and desired also to construct a dwelling among the people, that he might be near to protect and serve them should trouble arise again. Janthar loved his father deeply and held an unwavering confidence in the king's love for him. He had no doubt that his request would be granted. His appearance before the throne was not born of necessity, but of honor; a reverent formality. In his heart, he already possessed what he sought.

The throne room itself responded to the hearts of those who entered. Great torches lined its walls, their flames brightening in joy or dimming in sorrow. As Janthar stepped into the hall, the torches flared brilliantly, as though welcoming him with radiant approval; a manifestation of his own disposition. The king's magistrates stood in silent reverence as the prince approached the throne with boldness and respect. He bowed low before his father, then made his request with clarity and confidence.

King Orelian beamed with delight.

"Yes, my son! You already have the thing you have asked of me, for your heart has received it through expectation."

Joyfully, Janthar bowed once more and departed, already preparing the materials he knew were coming.

Soon after, the firstborn son entered. But unlike his younger brother, he brought with him a shadow of suspicion. The torches that had glowed so brightly now dimmed, casting long and somber silhouettes across the room. Prince Doombar, too, sought supplies to rebuild and hoped to build a home for himself. But unlike Janthar, he doubted his father's willingness to bless him personally. He believed the king would support the restoration of others, but questioned whether he was worthy of such goodness for himself.

He approached the throne with a semblance of reverence, but it was a posture born of fear, not trust. He offered only a half-bow, his eyes avoiding his father's. His expression betrayed a wounded heart one unsure of the love it so desperately needed. With trembling voice, he presented his request, wavering between the calling of sonship and the sorrow of feeling unworthy to bear it. The sight pained King Orelian. He paused in solemn silence as his magistrates held their breath.

Then the king spoke, his voice heavy with sorrow:

"Oh my son, how greatly you are loved yet you cannot see it. Be it unto you according to your expectation: you shall have the supplies for others, but not the home for yourself."

Doombar's face darkened. He turned swiftly and stormed out, his heart inflamed with offense. He could not comprehend that the kingdom's law, unshifting and true, had merely honored the belief he carried. The king remained on his throne, eyes full of tears. He wept not only for his son, but for the many like him. How deeply he desires to pour out blessings upon them all, yet his hands are bound by the very expectations they cling to.

So it is with us in the Kingdom of Heaven. It is governed by spiritual law: what we release is what we receive. If we release from our hearts forgiveness, we will be forgiven. If we financially give, finances will be given to us. If we encourage others, we ourselves will be encouraged. If we are slow to rash judgement, then we will not be judged by the standard we used. If we show mercy, mercy will be shown to us. The converse of all these things are true as well. We receive not only according to what we speak, but according to what we give out and what we truly believe in our hearts.

Mark 9:23 *"What do you mean, 'If I can'?" Jesus asked. "Anything is possible if a person believes."*

Light for the Path

In God's Kingdom, we receive in proportion to what we truly believe and expect in our hearts. Faith opens the door to His abundance, while doubt limits what we can experience of His goodness.

Deeper Light – Reflect + Respond

1. Read More

- Mark 11:22–26
- Matthew 5:7, 7:1–5, 9:20-30
- Luke 6:37–38
- James 1:5–8
- Proverbs 11:25
- Hebrews 11:6

2. Journal Prompt

- In what areas of my life do I believe God will bless others but struggle to believe He will bless me personally?
- Have I been approaching God like Prince Janthar, with trust and honor, or like Prince Doombar, with suspicion and fear?
- How would my prayers change if I truly believed God delights to give me what aligns with His will?

3. Daily Declaration of Faith

"I believe my Father delights to bless me, and I receive all He has promised. I walk by faith, not by doubt, knowing that what I expect of Him, I will surely see come to pass."

4. Live It Out

- This week, bring a specific request to God and thank Him daily as though you've already received it.
- Speak words of faith over your life and circumstances.
- Intentionally give encouragement, mercy, or generosity to someone, trusting that you will reap what you sow.

Reflection

_____

_____

_____

_____

_____

_____

_____

_____

_____

_____

_____

_____

_____

_____

_____

_____

_____

_____

_____

_____

Week 3

But God

"But God" are two words that can change anything.

Ephesians 2:4–5 (NLT) *"**But God** is so rich in mercy, and He loved us so much, that even though we were dead because of our sins, He gave us life when He raised Christ from the dead."*

Any difficulty or impossibility can be overcome with just those two simple words. The challenges we face in this life often seem insurmountable. But everything begins to change when we shift our focus to the limitlessness of God. Scripture reminds us that nothing is too hard for Him.

Jeremiah 32:17 (NLT) *"O Sovereign Lord! You made the heavens and earth by your strong hand and powerful arm. Nothing is too hard for you!"*

When we begin declaring the truth about who God is and what He can do in the midst of our circumstances, everything starts to shift. Our perspective changes, and we are lifted from the pit to the mountaintop. Joy becomes the fuel that produces strength.

Nehemiah 8:10 (NLT) *"Don't be dejected and sad, for the joy of the Lord is your strength!"*

Try adding the words "but God" to any problem or situation you are facing. Watch as faith, joy, and strength begin to rise within you. God's Word works every time.

Isaiah 55:11 (NLT) *"It is the same with my word. I send it out, and it always produces fruit. It will accomplish all I want it to, and it will prosper everywhere I send it."*

The limitlessness of God helps us take our eyes off what is seen and focus on what is unseen. When our hearts and minds are filled with what God can do, we step into a place of great faith and hope. The things that once seemed impossible begin to shift with a simple declaration: "But God." He will never fail or disappoint.

1 Peter 2:6 (AMP) *"...he who believes in Him [who adheres to, trusts in, and relies on Him] will never be disappointed [in his expectations]."*

Light for the Path

Two small words, **But God**, can change everything. They shift our focus from impossibility to God's limitless power, filling us with faith, joy, and strength to overcome.

Deeper Light – Reflect + Respond

1. Read More

- Genesis 50:20
- Psalm 73:26
- Jeremiah 32:17
- Romans 8:28
- Isaiah 55:10–11

2. Journal Prompt

- What situation in my life right now needs a But God declaration spoken over it?
- How does shifting my perspective to God's limitlessness change the way I feel about my challenges?
- What past situations has God already turned around for my good?

3. Daily Declaration of Faith

"No matter what I face, I declare, "But God." His mercy has made me alive, His joy is my strength, and His Word never fails. Nothing is too hard for my God, and I will never be disappointed when I put my trust in Him."

4. **Live It Out**

- Write down your top three current challenges and add But God next to each one as a declaration of faith.
- Share a testimony with someone this week of a time God turned your situation around.
- Each morning, speak a But God statement over your day before you begin.
- Declare, "No matter what I face, I know that these two powerful and simple words, "but God," will lead me in the right direction. My eyes are on the limitlessness of God.

Reflection:

_____

_____

_____

_____

_____

_____

_____

_____

_____

_____

_____

_____

_____

_____

_____

_____

_____

Week 4

Paid in FULL: Nothing Missing, Nothing Broken

I Corinthians 11:29–30 *"For he who eats and drinks in an unworthy manner eats and drinks judgment to himself, not discerning the Lord's body. For this reason many are weak and sick among you, and many sleep."*

Many believers struggle with understanding the meaning of the phrase "not discerning the Lord's body." Yet the very next verse brings clarity: "…many are weak and sick among you." The apostle Paul is essentially revealing that many believers do not receive physical healing because they do not understand the full extent of what was accomplished through the body of Christ; His body was broken so that our broken bodies might be made whole.

To bring clarity, consider this Old Testament principle:

Leviticus 24:20 *"Fracture for fracture, eye for eye, tooth for tooth; as he has caused disfigurement of a man, so shall it be done to him."*

While we no longer live under the law in a religious or ritualistic sense, it still reveals the unchanging justice and nature of God. Here, God is saying that if a man harms another, he must bear the consequence in like manner: eye for eye, tooth for tooth. But the converse of this is also true. If someone has a damaged eye and seeks restoration, then someone with a whole eye must be wounded on their behalf. If someone has a broken tooth and desires healing, then a whole tooth must be sacrificed.

Exodus 21:25 *"Burn for burn, wound for wound, **stripe for stripe.**"*

Jesus, in His perfect and healthy body, took upon Himself the stripes and wounds meant for us so that we could receive healing. That's why

Isaiah declares, *"By His stripes we are healed"* (**Isaiah 53:5**). But this truth doesn't stop at the physical level; it goes even deeper.

Isaiah 53:11 NASB *"As a result of the **anguish of His soul**, He will see it and be satisfied; By His knowledge the Righteous One, My Servant, will justify the many, For He will bear their wrongdoings."*

Jesus endured soul crushing anguish in the Garden of Gethsemane so that our souls could be restored to wholeness.

Matthew 26:38 *"Then He said to them, 'My soul is exceedingly sorrowful, even to death. Stay here and watch with Me.'"*

Remember God's law: eye for eye, tooth for tooth. Or in fuller form: body for body, soul for soul, spirit for spirit. Jesus bore the anguish of our souls that we might walk in soul level healing and peace. And on the cross, we see the spiritual cost:

Mark 15:34 *"And at the ninth hour Jesus cried out with a loud voice, saying, 'Eloi, Eloi, lama sabachthani?' which is translated, 'My God, My God, why have You forsaken Me?'"*

For the first time in eternity, Jesus experienced spiritual separation from the Father. Why? Because He became sin, and sin separates us from God (**2 Corinthians 5:21; Isaiah 59:2**). That spiritual disconnection was a real and painful death so that we would never again be spiritually separated from God.

I fully believe that after Jesus' physical death, He descended to hell to suffer and rose again three days later. This truth is symbolized in the Passover instructions: the lamb was not only to be slaughtered, but also burned (**Exodus 12:10**) and Christ is our Passover Lamb (**1 Corinthians 5:7**).

Psalm 16:10 confirms this: *"You will not leave my soul in Sheol."*

Jesus was spiritually separated so that we never would be. His soul was crushed with sorrow so that ours could be healed. His body was broken so that our bodies could be restored. Every part of Him—spirit, soul, and body—was offered up to make every part of us whole.

So, are you in need of healing today? In your body? In your soul or heart? In your spirit?

It has already been paid for in full by Jesus Christ. But remember: all things from God are received by faith. We believe, and then we speak (**2 Corinthians 4:13**). So declare it:

Speak to the sickness and command it to leave your body!

Speak to the wounds in your soul and command them to be restored!

Command every lying spirit whispering separation or condemnation to be silenced and cast out!

You are not separated, you are eternally connected to Him.

Just as Eve was taken out of Adam and formed, and Adam declared:

Genesis 2:23 *"This is now bone of my bones and flesh of my flesh."*

So now our Savior declares the same of us:

Ephesians 5:30 *"For we are members of His body, of His flesh and of His bones."*

We are of Him, from Him, and for Him. Everything we need for complete wholeness—spirit, soul, and body—has already been provided in Christ.

So let us join in the heavenly chorus:

Revelation 5:12–13 *"Worthy is the Lamb who was slain To receive power and riches and wisdom, And strength and honor and glory and blessing!" Blessing and honor and glory and power Be to Him who sits on the throne, And to the Lamb, forever and ever!"*

Light for the Path

Through His body, soul, and spirit, Jesus paid in full for our complete wholeness. Healing, restoration, and reconciliation with God are already ours—spirit, soul, and body—received by faith.

Deeper Light – Reflect + Respond

1. Read More

- Isaiah 53:4–5
- Matthew 8:16–17
- 2 Peter 1:2-4
- Hebrews 10:19–22
- 2 Corinthians 5:21

2. Journal Prompt

- Which area of my life; body, soul, or spirit; needs to experience the wholeness Jesus purchased for me?
- Have I been accepting brokenness in any area instead of declaring the healing Jesus already paid for?
- How does understanding that Jesus bore it all for me change my approach to prayer and faith?

3. Daily Declaration of Faith

"Every part of me, spirit, soul, and body, has been made whole through Jesus. His body was broken for my healing, His soul was crushed for my peace, and His Spirit bore separation so I could be forever united with God. I live in complete wholeness, paid in full by the blood of the Lamb."

4. Live It Out

- Speak declarations of healing over the specific area lacking the manifestation; body, soul, or spirit; each day this week.
- Take communion intentionally, meditating on the wholeness Jesus purchased for you.
- Share with someone the truth that Christ paid for complete restoration, and offer to pray for them.

Reflection

Week 5

THE BLOOD!

Hebrews 10:14 (MSG) *"It was a perfect sacrifice by a perfect person to perfect some very imperfect people."*

Raise your hand if you fall into the "very imperfect" people group! Thanks to the perfect sacrifice of a perfect person, you no longer have to stay in that category. That perfect person is Jesus Christ.

The Bible makes it clear that the blood of animals could never bring perfect cleansing for those who came to worship God (**Hebrews 10:1 NLT**). Under the Old Covenant, these sacrifices had to be offered again and again, year after year, and they served only as a reminder to the worshippers of the sins that still required atonement (**Hebrews 10:3 NLT**).

But the blood of Jesus did what no animal sacrifice could ever do. His blood didn't just cover sin, it removed it entirely, along with the guilt and shame that came with it. That's a reason to rise up and celebrate! Jesus purchased our freedom from death, sin, shame, and guilt with His powerful, unblemished blood. His blood was the key that unlocked the prison of sin we were trapped in.

Under the New Covenant, our sacrifices to Him are no longer about making atonement for sin. They are acts of love, gratitude, and obedience to the One who paid the ultimate price on our behalf.

Hebrews 8:6 (AMPC) *"But as it now is, He [Christ] has acquired a [priestly] ministry which is as much superior and more excellent [than the old] as the covenant (the agreement) of which He is the Mediator (the Arbiter, Agent) is superior and more excellent, [because] it is enacted and rests upon more important (sublimer, higher, and nobler) promises."*

We are now called to recognize the *enormity* of what the blood of Jesus accomplished, not only for ourselves but also for the sake of those around us.

> **Matthew 28:19 (NLT)** *"Go therefore and make disciples of all the nations, baptizing them in the name of the Father and of the Son and of the Holy Spirit."*

Live free from the guilt, shame, and punishment of sin by fully receiving all that the blood of Jesus purchased for you.

Light for the Path

The blood of Jesus did what no other sacrifice could; removing sin completely and breaking the power of guilt and shame. It purchased our freedom and gave us a new life of righteousness.

Deeper Light – Reflect + Respond

1. Read More

- Hebrews 9:11–14
- 1 Peter 1:18–19
- Romans 5:8–9
- Revelation 1:5–6
- Isaiah 1:18

2. Journal Prompt

- Have I been living as though I'm still bound by guilt or shame, even though Jesus' blood has set me free?
- How can I more intentionally share the power of the blood of Jesus with others this week?
- What areas of my life need a fresh reminder that His sacrifice was "once for all"?

3. Daily Declaration of Faith

"By the blood of Jesus, my sin, guilt, and shame are gone forever; I am free, forgiven, and walking in the power of His New Covenant promises."

4. Live It Out

- Each day this week, thank Jesus specifically for something His blood has accomplished in your life.
- Declare over your life; "I have been made righteous in the eyes of God, not because of anything I have done, but because of everything Jesus has already done for me!" 2 Corinthians 5:21
- Memorize Hebrews 10:14 as a daily reminder of your standing before God.

Reflection

_____

_____

_____

_____

_____

_____

_____

_____

_____

_____

_____

_____

_____

_____

_____

_____

_____

_____

_____

Week 6

THE BRIDGE

Luke 15:20 *"And he arose and came to his father. But when he was still a great way off, his father saw him and had compassion, and ran and fell on his neck and kissed him."*

Recently, during a time of intercessory prayer, I received a vision from the Lord of two trees with a bridge connecting them. I didn't understand its meaning until I received revelation on the above verse.

In the story of the prodigal son, the son took his share of his father's inheritance and squandered it in worldly living. Eventually, he found himself destitute and barely surviving. Recognizing his poor choices, he decided to return home, planning to apologize and ask for a menial job from his father.

What he encountered instead revealed the unconditional love of a father. His father saw him while he was still far away, ran to him, embraced him, and welcomed him back home. It wasn't about what the son had done wrong; it was about his return and the restoration of a son to his father. This is the heart of God the Father and the mission of Jesus the Son.

The bridge I saw in the vision was a symbol of the sacrificed life of Jesus. He is the bridge that allows the human race to return home to the Father. No longer held down by bad choices, but washed clean and set free by the blood of the One who made the way.

Hebrews 10:19-20 (NLT) *"And so, dear brothers and sisters, we can boldly enter heaven's Most Holy Place because of the blood of Jesus. By his death, Jesus opened a new and life-giving way through the curtain into the Most Holy Place."*

Just as the prodigal son's father welcomed him home with no questions asked, God the Father gave His one and only Son—Jesus—to do the same for us. Jesus bridged the gap between the holiness of God and the brokenness of humanity, making a way for us to return home fully accepted, completely forgiven, and embraced without hesitation.

If you have not crossed that bridge yet, today is your day. Cross the bridge and come home to your Father who has been waiting for you.

Light for the Path

Jesus is the bridge between our brokenness and the Father's holiness. Through His sacrifice, we can return home fully accepted, completely forgiven, and embraced without hesitation.

Deeper Light – Reflect + Respond

1. Read More

- John 14:6
- 1 Timothy 2:5–6
- Ephesians 2:13–18
- Colossians 1:19–22
- Hebrews 4:14–16

2. Journal Prompt

- Have I personally crossed the "bridge" of Jesus into full relationship with the Father, or am I still standing at a distance?
- What holds me back from receiving God's embrace as the prodigal son did?
- How can I help others find and cross the bridge into God's presence?

3. Daily Declaration of Faith

"Through Jesus, my bridge to the Father, I am fully accepted, completely forgiven, and forever embraced in His love."

4. **Live It Out**

- Take time this week to thank Jesus for being the bridge that reconciled you to God.
- Share your testimony with someone who needs to know that God welcomes them home.
- Meditate on Luke 15:20 and picture the Father running toward you with joy.

Reflection

Week 7

The Debt Has Been Paid

Mark 11:26 *"But if you do not forgive, neither will your Father in heaven forgive your trespasses."*

To harbor unforgiveness is to hold out an invoice, demanding payment for a wrong done against you. How arrogant it is to insist that others pay a debt for their sins against us when we ourselves were incapable of paying our own. If we were helpless to atone for our transgressions, what makes us think others are capable of atoning for theirs?

Here's the truth we must grasp deeply:

Jesus didn't only die for our sins, He also died for the sins committed against us.

Yes, even the deepest wounds. Even the violations that pierced your soul and left you bleeding inside. He bore all of it. Every injustice, every betrayal, every harm, you name it. The wrath and punishment we believe our offenders deserve was poured out on Him.

It is as if Jesus Himself says:

"I saw the pain. The trauma. The tears. And I allowed the Father to punish Me for those very wrongs as if I had committed them. The justice you longed for, I absorbed into My body. I endured the full weight of wrath so you would no longer have to carry the desire for vengeance."

To hold onto unforgiveness, then, is to say His sacrifice wasn't enough. It's to lift up a debt ledger before the cross and whisper, "This still hasn't been paid." But beloved, it has been paid. In full! There's no more payment needed. Not from them. Not from you. Not from anyone.

John 2:2 *"And He Himself is the propitiation for our sins, and not for ours only but also for the whole world."*

Every offense, believer and unbeliever alike, was answered at Calvary.

Unforgiveness is more than just pain; it's pride. It puts us in the judge's seat, above the law, above the cross, even above Christ. But who among us is righteous enough to judge? Who is pure enough to enforce perfect justice?

James speaks to this heart:

James 4:11 *"He who speaks evil of a brother and judges his brother, speaks evil of the law and judges the law… But if you judge the law, you are not a doer of the law but a judge."*

We are not fit to judge the law. We couldn't keep it so how could we enforce it?

The burden of judgment is not ours to carry. We are invited instead to rest, to lay down the weight of unforgiveness, of demanding justice, and enter the freedom Christ purchased.

Mark 12:31 *"You shall love your neighbor as yourself."*

This is the way of the Kingdom: love that keeps no record of wrongs. A life loosed from the chains of bitterness, pride, and pain. A heart unoffended. A soul free.

One of the greatest hindrances to spiritual growth is unforgiveness because it feels justified. That sense of justification is pride in disguise. It says, "I am qualified to hold this against you." But we are not. We must give what we've received: forgiveness. Freely. Entirely.

To love like Christ is to say:

"You owe me nothing. Not for yesterday's wounds, and not for tomorrow's offenses. The cross of Christ was more than enough."

And remember this: The person who relates to God through works will always struggle with forgiveness. Why? Because striving and withholding go hand in hand.

Condemnation is simply unforgiveness turned inward, self-judgment, self-striving, self-rejection. It's pride in another form.

To receive grace is to stop striving.

To rest in forgiveness is to stop judging.

You cannot earn righteousness and you cannot enforce it on others.

You must fall at the feet of Mercy.

Mark 8:35 *"For whoever desires to save his life will lose it, but whoever loses his life for My sake and the gospel's will save it."*

The way of freedom is the way of surrender. Let the cross be enough for you and for them. The debt has been paid.

Light for the Path

Forgiveness releases the debtor because the debt was already paid in full by Jesus. When we let go of unforgiveness, we step out of the judge's seat and into the freedom Christ purchased.

Deeper Light – Reflect + Respond

1. Read More

- Matthew 18:21–35
- Colossians 3:12–14
- Romans 12:17–21
- Psalm 103:10–14
- Ephesians 4:31–32

2. Journal Prompt

- Is there anyone I still hold an "invoice" against, expecting them to make things right?
- How does realizing that Jesus died for the sins committed against me change my view of those who hurt me?
- In what ways might pride be disguising itself as my "right" to stay offended?

3. Daily Declaration of Faith

"The cross is enough. Every debt against me was paid in full by Jesus. I release all unforgiveness and choose to walk in freedom, love, and mercy, just as I have received."

4. **Live It Out**

- Write down the names of people you've struggled to forgive and pray over each one, releasing them to God.
- Speak aloud, "You owe me nothing," as an act of faith and freedom.
- Spend time meditating on 1 John 2:2, thanking Jesus for His complete sacrifice.

Reflection

_____

_____

_____

_____

_____

_____

_____

_____

_____

_____

_____

_____

_____

_____

_____

_____

_____

_____

_____

_____

_____

Week 8

Spirit, Soul, and Body

1 Thessalonians 5:23 *"Now may the God of peace Himself sanctify you completely; and may your whole spirit, soul, and body be preserved blameless at the coming of our Lord Jesus Christ."*

God created man in His image and likeness. Just as God manifests Himself in three persons—God the Father, God the Son, and God the Holy Spirit—He likewise created man in three parts: spirit, soul, and body. The truest part of who we are is our spirit, which is eternal. We also have a soul, made up of our mind, will, and emotions. We live in a body, which is the tent that houses both the spirit and soul.

Without this foundational understanding, many Christians can become confused or even frustrated when reading the Bible, as some verses may appear to contradict one another.

We must recognize that salvation has taken place in our spirit. Our soul and body, however, are not yet fully redeemed, though our spirit has been sealed by the Holy Spirit until the day of redemption when the salvation of the spirit will fully flood the soul and body (see Ephesians 1:13–14).

1 Corinthians 6:17 *"But he who is joined to the Lord is one spirit with Him."*

While our spirit is already united with Christ, our soul is undergoing the process of sanctification:

Hebrews 10:14 *"For by one offering He has perfected forever those who are being sanctified."*

The word "perfected" speaks of something completed, while "being sanctified" speaks of something ongoing. How can both be true at the same time? The answer lies in understanding that our spirit has been perfected, completed at salvation, while our soul is still in process. Sanctification progresses as our soul aligns with our spirit. When this alignment happens, revelation flows, and the truth already present in our spirit begins to govern our soul. The soul then becomes a conduit through which the power of the spirit can flow and manifest outwardly.

Everything we need already exists in our spirit:

2 Peter 1:2–3 *"Grace and peace be multiplied to you in the knowledge of God and of Jesus our Lord, as His divine power has given to us all things that pertain to life and godliness, through the knowledge of Him who called us by glory and virtue."*

Ephesians 1:3 *"Blessed be the God and Father of our Lord Jesus Christ, who has blessed us with every spiritual blessing in the heavenly places in Christ."*

So remember: your spirit is joined to Christ and made perfect— nothing more is needed there! Your responsibility now is to bring the perfection of your spirit into the realm of your soul. This is the journey of sanctification and the pathway to inner wholeness. As your soul comes into agreement with your spirit, you will begin to live, speak, and act like Jesus.

This is the heart of the gospel, for Jesus Himself said that after declaring the gospel, its first function was to heal the heart;

Luke 4:18a *"The Spirit of the Lord is upon Me, because He has anointed Me To preach the gospel to the poor; He has sent Me to* **heal the brokenhearted…"**

Light for the Path

Your spirit was perfected at salvation, your soul is being sanctified, and your body will one day be fully redeemed. Yet, as your soul aligns with your spirit, you can now experience the life of Christ within you, as it flows outward into every part of who you are.

Deeper Light – Reflect + Respond

1. Read More

- Romans 12:1–2
- 2 Corinthians 4:16–18
- Hebrews 4:12
- Romans 6:4-11
- Ephesians 4:22–24

2. Journal Prompt

- Do I primarily identify with my spirit (the truest me) or with my soul and body?
- What areas of my soul-my mind, will, or emotions-need to come into greater agreement with the truth of my perfected spirit?
- How does understanding this three-part design change the way I read Scripture and live daily?

3. Daily Declaration of Faith

"My spirit is one with Christ and already perfected. As my soul aligns with my spirit, the life of God flows through me, bringing wholeness to my mind, emotions, and body."

4. Live It Out

- Take one verse about your identity in Christ and meditate on it daily, letting it renew your mind.
- When emotions or thoughts don't align with God's Word, speak out the truth that already exists in your spirit.
- Dedicate your body to God this week through acts of service, healthy stewardship, and purity.

Reflection

_____

_____

_____

_____

_____

_____

_____

_____

_____

_____

_____

_____

_____

_____

_____

_____

_____

_____

_____

KNOWLEDGE > FEELINGS

God's love is not a feeling; it is the unshakable truth that He loves us regardless of our circumstances or emotions. His desire for His children is not that we *pursue* the feeling of His love, but that we find comfort and encouragement in the unwavering knowledge that His love remains with us always.

Definition of constant:

Occurring continuously or regularly over a period of time; persistent.

Unchanging in nature, value, or extent; consistent or steady.

Faithful and dependable; loyal.

God's love is all of these: continuous, unchanging, faithful, and dependable. His love is everlasting and unfailing. If your experience of His love feels inconsistent or conditional, you may be chasing a feeling rather than standing on the firm foundation of truth.

Jeremiah 31:3 (NLT) *"Long ago the LORD said to Israel: 'I have loved you, my people, with an everlasting love. With unfailing love I have drawn you to myself.'"*

This pursuit of emotional highs is what keeps some of God's sons and daughters in a roller-coaster relationship with Him. When they feel His love or sense His nearness, all is well. But when life gets difficult and those tangible feelings fade, they begin to question His presence. Doubts creep in. They wonder if God has abandoned them or stopped loving them.

Roller coasters may be thrilling, but the ride is short. And the same is true for a relationship built on emotional experiences alone. God did not design our walk with Him to be dictated by our feelings. He designed a life in which we are anchored in the certainty of His love, whether we feel it or not, whether we see it or not.

Hebrews 13:5 *"Let your conduct be without covetousness; be content with such things as you have. For He Himself has said, 'I will never leave you nor forsake you.'"*

Romans 5:8 *"But God showed His great love for us by sending Christ to die for us while we were still sinners."*

God gave His only Son for us, not because we were lovable, but because *He is love*. His love does not ebb and flow like human affection; it is steadfast, trustworthy, and eternal. While we were still sinners, He loved us, and that love has never changed.

So, the next time you are tempted to get back on the roller coaster, chasing the feeling of His love, remember what His Word says: His love is continuous, eternal, and unfailing. Do not get back on that ride. Stand firm in the knowledge that His love is in you and with you forever.

Light for the Path

God's love is constant; unchanging, faithful, and everlasting. Our confidence rests in the truth of His Word, not in fluctuating emotions or circumstances.

Deeper Light – Reflect + Respond

1. Read More

- 2 Corinthians 5:7
- Isaiah 54:10
- John 15:9–10
- Romans 8:35–39
- 1 John 4:9–10

2. Journal Prompt

- Have I been relying on feelings to measure God's love for me?
- What truths from Scripture can I hold onto when my emotions tell me God is distant?
- How can I build a steadier walk with God that's anchored in knowledge rather than feelings?

3. Daily Declaration of Faith

"God's love for me is everlasting, unfailing, and constant. I do not live by feelings, but by the truth of His Word: He will never leave me nor forsake me."

4. **Live It Out**

- Memorize Jeremiah 31:3 and Hebrews 13:5 as anchors for your faith.
- When emotions fluctuate, declare God's promises aloud until your thoughts align with His truth.
- Keep a gratitude journal to record ways God's love has been evident in your life, even in difficult times.

Reflection

_____

_____

_____

_____

_____

_____

_____

_____

_____

_____

_____

_____

_____

_____

_____

_____

_____

_____

_____

You Are Not Your Flesh: Part 1

One of the major shifts that must take place in the life of every believer in order to walk in dominion is learning to no longer see yourself in the flesh, but in the Spirit. You must live each day fully aware of your new existence, being joined to Christ. Many believers struggle with this truth because they still feel temptations to sin from time to time. This struggle has led to the erroneous belief that believers have two natures: a sin nature and a regenerated nature. But nothing could be further from the truth! And if you believe this error, you will remain bound by the law of sin your entire life.

I have good news, the revelation in this devotion can set you free!

Let's go back to the beginning:

Genesis 2:16-17 *"And the Lord God commanded the man, saying, 'Of every tree of the garden you may freely eat; but of the tree of the knowledge of good and evil you shall not eat, for in the day that you eat of it you shall surely die.'"*

Before Adam ate from the tree, he enjoyed unhindered communion with God. He was connected to God in spirit—his source of life—for Adam did not become a living, self-aware being until God breathed His Spirit into his formed body.

Let me ask you a question: did Adam physically die the day he ate the fruit? Of course not, he went on to live 930 years after that moment. So, did God lie when He warned Adam that he would die the day he ate the fruit? Absolutely not! For God cannot lie (**Hebrews 6:18**). Most believers would agree that Adam died spiritually the day he sinned. Death, in its simplest form, is separation and God is the source of life. So, when Adam sinned, he became spiritually dead, severed from the Life that once filled his spirit.

Psalm 36:9 *"For with You is the fountain (source) of life; In Your light we see light."* (Insert mine)

Isaiah 59:2 *"But your iniquities have separated you from your God; And your sins have hidden His face from you, So that He will not hear."*

Let me ask you another question: was Adam a sinner before he ate the fruit? Certainly not! Adam did not become a sinner until he disobeyed God and spiritually died. From that moment on, every person born from Adam inherited that dead, sinful nature.

Genesis 5:3 *"And Adam lived one hundred and thirty years, and begot a son in his own likeness, after his image (sinful nature), and named him Seth."* (Insert mine)

Romans 5:12 *"Therefore, just as through one man sin entered the world, and death through sin, and thus death spread to all men, because all sinned."*

I pose these questions not to be rhetorical, but to provoke logical and spiritual reflection. Since Adam was sinless while his spirit was alive and connected to God, and sin entered only after he disobeyed, which caused his spirit to die, we can conclude this: our nature is determined by the condition of our spirit.

Here's the powerful truth:

When our spirit is alive and connected to God, we do not have a sin nature. When our spirit is dead and separated from Him, we do.

Said another way: **As the spirit of a man goes, so goes the rest of the man**. When Adam sinned, his spirit died, and that death extended to his soul and body.

However, those who have received salvation through the death and resurrection of Jesus Christ have been given a "born again" spirit. Our spirits are no longer dead but are now alive and reconnected to God!

1 Corinthians 6:17 *"But he who is joined to the Lord is one spirit with Him."*

John 3:5 *"Jesus answered, "Most assuredly, I say to you, unless one is born of water and the Spirit, he cannot enter the kingdom of God."*

Colossians 2:13 *"And you, being dead in your trespasses and the uncircumcision of your flesh, He has made alive together with Him, having forgiven you all trespasses."*

John 17:22–23 *"And the glory which You gave Me I have given them, that they may be one just as We are one: I in them, and You in Me; that they may be made perfect in one, and that the world may know that You have sent Me, and have loved them as You have loved Me."*

We have a saying in my house that goes like this: "If Life is in my spirit, sickness cannot be in my body." (**Romans 8:11**). As believers with born again spirits, we can now confidently expect the life within our spirits to overflow into our souls and bodies.

Therefore, we no longer have a sin nature! We are alive and united with God in perfect communion through the Spirit of Christ.

Now, some might wonder: "If we no longer have a sin nature, where do the seeming impulses to sin come from?"

Let's discuss that truth in the Part 2.

Light for the Path

Your nature is determined by the condition of your spirit. In Christ, your spirit is alive, united with Him, and free from the sin nature; empowered for life, not bondage.

Deeper Light – Reflect + Respond

1. Read More

- Romans 6:4–7
- Galatians 2:20
- 2 Corinthians 5:17–18
- John 3:3–6
- Romans 8:10–11

2. Journal Prompt

- How does knowing I no longer have a sin nature change the way I see myself?
- Have I been identifying more with my past (dead spirit) or my present reality in Christ (born again spirit)?
- What areas of my life still need to come under the influence of the Life in my spirit?

3. Daily Declaration of Faith

"I no longer have a sin nature. My spirit is alive and joined to Christ, and the life of God in me overflows into my soul and body."

4. Live It Out

- Begin each day declaring, "I am alive in Christ, and my spirit is one with His."
- When tempted, remind yourself that your nature is not sinful; you are a new creation in Christ.
- Study Romans 6–8 this week, noting every verse that affirms your new life in the Spirit.

Reflection

_____
_____
_____
_____
_____
_____
_____
_____
_____
_____
_____
_____
_____
_____
_____
_____
_____
_____

You are Not Your Flesh: Part 2

So, where do these *seemingly* uncontrollable impulses to sin come from? If we no longer have a sin nature compelling us, why do some believers still struggle with sin?

The answer is twofold: because sin still resides in our flesh and in the un-renewed parts of our mind.

Let's examine a well known passage of Scripture that has often been used to support the mistaken belief that believers have two natures. This interpretation, however, stems from a misunderstanding of the text.

Romans 7:15–18 *"For what I am doing, I do not understand. For what I will to do, that I do not practice; but what I hate, that I do. If, then, I do what I will not to do, I agree with the law that it is good. But now, it is no longer I who do it, but sin that dwells in me. For I know that in me (that is, in my flesh) nothing good dwells; for to will is present with me, but how to perform what is good I do not find."*

Here, Paul expresses deep frustration over his inability to overcome sin. But was he describing a present struggle, or reflecting on a past one? I believe Paul was referring to a past struggle for several reasons. First, look at this earlier statement in the same chapter:

Romans 7:5 *"For **when** we were **in the flesh**, the sinful passions which were aroused by the law were at work in our members to bear fruit to death."*

Paul uses the past tense, **"when we were in the flesh"** indicating that what follows describes a condition that no longer applies to the believer. Then, in the very next chapter, Paul makes it even clearer:

Romans 8:9 *"But you are **not in the flesh but in the Spirit**, if indeed the Spirit of God dwells in you. Now if anyone does not have the Spirit of Christ, he is not His."*

Those who have the Spirit of God living in them are no longer in the flesh, but in the Spirit. That is a critical distinction. Therefore, I believe that in **Romans 7**, Paul is recalling his life before he belonged to Christ, when he lived under the law and lacked the power to overcome sin.

Revisiting **Romans 7:18**:

*"For I know that in me (that is, in my flesh) nothing good dwells; for **to will** is present with me, but **how** to perform what is good **I do not find**."*

Paul acknowledges the desire to do good, but also a total lack of ability to carry it out because he was a slave to the sinful tendencies of the flesh. Then he reaches a turning point:

Romans 7:24–25a *"O wretched man that I am! Who will deliver me from this body of death? I thank God through Jesus Christ our Lord!"*

Now, being in Christ, Paul has access to the very power he once lacked, the power to rule over the flesh and do what is truly good. He is no longer bound to the ***"body of death."*** Since death is the result of sin, Paul is declaring that he now walks in victory over both sin and the death it brings.

Notice where he identifies sin as dwelling:

Romans 7:22–23 *"For I delight in the law of God according to the inward man. But I see another law **in my members**, warring against the law of my mind, and bringing me into captivity to the law of sin which is in my members."*

Sin still dwells in our **flesh**—not in our **spirit**. Now, as those who are in Christ, we have access, by faith, to God's grace and power, enabling us to dominate the flesh:

Romans 5:1–2 *"Therefore, having been justified by faith, we have peace with God through our Lord Jesus Christ, through whom also we have access by faith into this grace in which we stand…"*

Sin dwells in the flesh, and before salvation, our spirit was dead, offering no help in resisting the impulses of the flesh. In fact, it was that very dead spirit that propelled us toward the sin residing in our flesh. Now, having been joined to Christ, we possess the power to rule over our flesh, because the life within our spirit is greater than the sin that dwells in our flesh.

Light for the Path

Sin still resides in the flesh, but it no longer defines your nature. You must also go through the process of retraining your mind to think according to the new man. In Christ, your spirit is alive, and through His grace, you have the power to rule over the impulses of the flesh.

Deeper Light – Reflect + Respond

1. Read More

- Romans 6:6–14
- Galatians 5:16–17
- Colossians 3:1–10
- Titus 2:11–12
- 1 Peter 2:11

2. Journal Prompt

- In what areas do I still feel the pull of the flesh most strongly?
- How can I actively renew my mind so my thoughts align with my new nature in Christ?
- What steps can I take to rely more fully on God's grace when temptation comes?

3. Daily Declaration of Faith

"I am not my flesh. Sin may dwell in my body, but it no longer rules me. I live by the Spirit of God, and His power in me is greater than every impulse of the flesh. I walk in victory through Jesus Christ, my Lord."

4. **Live It Out**

- Identify one thought pattern or habit rooted in the flesh and replace it with a Spirit-led practice.
- When tempted, declare Romans 8:9 over yourself: "I am not in the flesh but in the Spirit."
- Spend time each day meditating on Scriptures that affirm your authority over sin through Christ.

Reflection

You are Not Your Flesh: Part 3

Now, we've come to the conclusion of our series: **the mind**.

When we are saved, our minds are not instantly and completely transformed. We still carry memories of our past lives and all the things we did before Christ. It's often these very memories that the enemy uses to try to keep us bound by shame, condemnation, guilt, and feelings of unworthiness. That's why it is essential that we go through the process of renewing our minds, so we may walk in alignment with our new spiritual nature in Christ.

Romans 12:2 *"And do not be conformed to this world, but be transformed by the renewing of your mind, that you may prove what is that good and acceptable and perfect will of God."*

This verse presents two realities, and one of them is always true in every life: we are either conforming or being transformed.

Conforming is effortless it requires no resistance. The world has a current, and if you don't intentionally push against it, it will pull you in. It tries to shape your identity through culture, the words of those closest to you and through your life experiences. But now, being in Christ, we are called to resist that current. We refuse to walk in the identity of our old selves.

2 Corinthians 5:7 *"For we walk by faith, not by sight."*

To walk successfully with God, we must embrace our new identity in Christ and reject the old identity rooted in the flesh. This is a journey of growth and spiritual maturity, one in which the Holy Spirit walks with us every step of the way, guiding us into truth.

John 14:26 *"But the Helper, the Holy Spirit, whom the Father will send in My name, He will teach you all things, and bring to your remembrance all things that I said to you."*

John 16:13 *"However, when He, the Spirit of truth, has come, He will guide you into all truth; for He will not speak on His own authority, but whatever He hears He will speak; and He will tell you things to come."*

Renewing the mind means literally changing the way we think. The Greek word for "renewing" means to renovate. Think of renovating a home; you remove the old to make way for the new. The updates are usually more efficient, more beautiful, and more restful. In the same way, when we align our thoughts with God's Word, we replace the old, broken ways of thinking with divine truth that brings peace, power, and purpose.

So how do we renew our minds?

Simply put: by reading and meditating on God's Word. Before Christ, our thought patterns were shaped by what we consistently heard and meditated upon. The same principle applies now, but instead of meditating on sin and worldly things, we now fill our minds with the Word of God.

Philippians 4:8 *"Finally, brethren, whatever things are true, whatever things are noble, whatever things are just, whatever things are pure, whatever things are lovely, whatever things are of good report, if there is any virtue and if there is anything praiseworthy meditate on these things."*

Colossians 3:2 AMPC *"And set your minds and keep them set on what is above (the higher things), not on the things that are on the earth."*

We are to fix our minds on what is true, and God's Word is truth (**John 17:17**). When we renew our minds, a miraculous transformation begins to unfold. The word "transformation" in **Romans 12:2** is the Greek word metamorphoō, from which we get our English word "metamorphosis." It means "to change the external form, to be transfigured, to undergo a spiritual transformation." This word is only used four times in the New Testament: **Matthew 17:1, Mark 9:2, 2 Corinthians 3:18, and Romans 12:2.**

Let's look at one of those powerful instances:

Matthew 17:1–2 *"Now after six days Jesus took Peter, James, and John his brother, led them up on a high mountain by themselves; and He was transfigured before them. His face shone like the sun, and His clothes became as white as the light."*

In this moment, also recorded in Mark's Gospel, the word is translated "transfigured." Jesus' body radiated light, and His clothing became dazzling white. It was a visible manifestation of the glory that was already within Him. His physical body couldn't contain the glory inside His Spirit, and it spilled outward in a radiant, tangible way.

Let me ask: did this glory descend upon Jesus in that moment, or was it already within Him? Clearly, it was already within. And here's the incredible truth: that same exact glory now lives within every born-again believer.

John 17:22 *"And the glory which You gave Me I have given them, that they may be one just as We are one:"*

We carry that same glory within our spirits, and the more we renew our minds to think like God, the more that glory will begin to shine through us on the outside. How else could we understand a verse like this:

John 14:12 *"Most assuredly, I say to you, he who believes in Me, the works that I do he will do also; and greater works than these he will do, because I go to My Father."*

It is the glory within us that empowers us to do the impossible. That glory becomes more visible in the life of every believer who chooses to transform their thinking. Because what you consistently meditate on fills your heart and what is in your heart will come out of your mouth.

Luke 6:45 / Matthew 12:34 *"For out of the abundance of the heart the mouth speaks."*

If you are meditating on sin, then sin and death will overflow from your lips. But if you are meditating on God's Word, then life and power will pour out. As you speak His Word, the supernatural glory of God, already inside you, will begin to manifest in your words, your actions, and your life as a whole. Yes, even your tongue will move mountains!

Light for the Path

Renewing your mind replaces old, broken thought patterns with God's truth, allowing the glory within your spirit to shine outward. As your thinking aligns with His Word, His life and power become visible in your actions, words, and daily walk.

Deeper Light – Reflect + Respond

1. Read More

- Romans 12:1–2
- 2 Corinthians 3:18
- Colossians 3:1–3
- Philippians 4:8–9
- John 17:22–23

2. Journal Prompt

- What old thought patterns still influence the way I see myself, God, or others?
- How would my daily life change if I truly believed that God's glory is already within me?
- What practical steps can I take to make God's Word the primary influence on my thinking?

3. Daily Declaration of Faith

"My mind is renewed daily by the Word of God. I fix my thoughts on what is true, pure, and eternal, and the glory of Christ within me shines outward in my words, actions, and life."

4. Live It Out

- Set aside time each day to meditate on a single verse, repeating it until it shapes your thinking.
- Speak God's promises out loud when old thought patterns try to resurface.
- Intentionally replace negative or flesh-driven speech with life-giving words rooted in Scripture.

Reflection

_____

_____

_____

_____

_____

_____

_____

_____

_____

_____

_____

_____

_____

_____

_____

_____

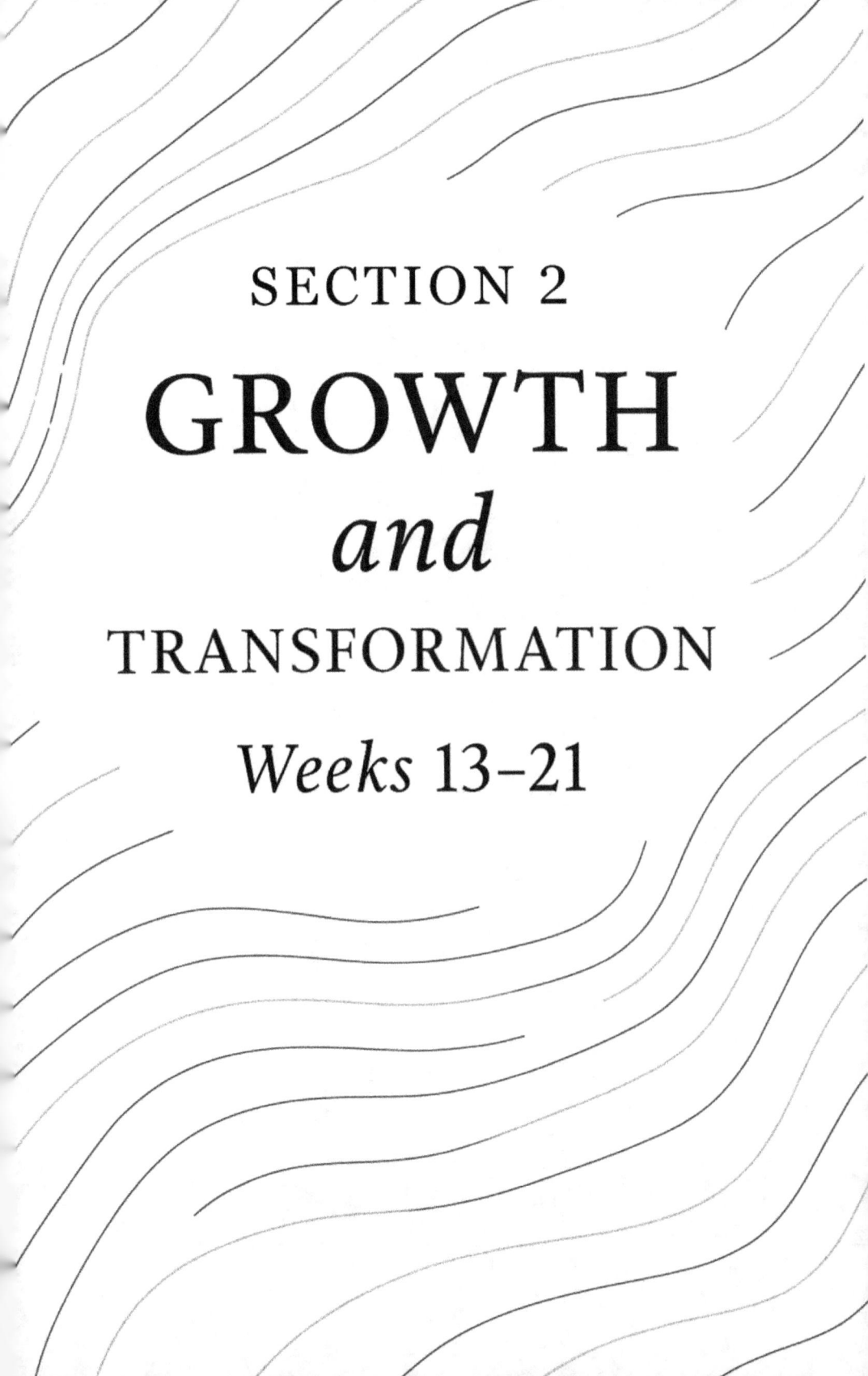

SECTION 2

GROWTH
and
TRANSFORMATION

Weeks 13–21

INSIDE OUT: NOT THE MOVIE

3 John 1:2 *"Beloved, I pray that you may prosper in all things and be in health, just as your soul prospers."*

God cares about ALL things that pertain to His greatest creation… humanity. He cares about our spirit, soul and body. He also designed us to prosper from the inside out, not from the outside in. He is our designer, and there is no one else who knows us better.

His perfect design is for us to prosper inwardly by growing in our relationship with Him through His Son, Jesus. Jesus is our direct connection to God. Thanks to Jesus, we have no excuse not to come boldly to the throne of grace whenever we want.

Hebrews 4:16 (MSG) *"So let's walk right up to him and get what he is so ready to give. Take the mercy, accept the help."*

Before you kick the word "prosperity" out of your vocabulary, let's define what it means. Prosperity is to thrive or advance in any given area. Or you could say in ALL given areas.

Prosperity is not a bad word. It's a word used in the Bible, inspired by the Holy Spirit, to show us what is available to all humanity through the blood of Jesus. According to **3 John 1:2**, it is literally the desire of our Good, Good Father for His children to prosper, to thrive, and to advance in every given area; spirit, soul, and body!

As we prosper inwardly, that prosperity begins to show outwardly. What we put into our bodies will eventually manifest on the outside of our bodies. That is just a fact, and the same is true for spiritual things.

What we plant into the soil of our hearts will eventually take root, grow, and bear fruit, whether good or bad. Watering the soil of our hearts with the Word of God will produce good fruit, while watering it with the things of this world will produce bad fruit. We all get to choose.

Deuteronomy 30:19 NLT *"Today I have given you the choice between life and death, between blessings and curses. Now I call on heaven and earth to witness the choice you make. Oh, that you would choose life, so that you and your descendants might live!"*

The bottom line is that it is God's desire for His children to prosper in **ALL things**. Those who have a heart for Him will make choices here on this earth that will produce prosperity in every area of their lives. This is what pleases and glorifies the Lord.

2 Corinthians 1:20 *"For all the promises of God in Him are Yes, and in Him Amen, to the glory of God through us."*

Light for the Path

God's design is for prosperity to start within, through a thriving soul connected to Him, and then flow outward into every area of life. When we plant His Word in our hearts, it produces fruit that glorifies Him and impacts every part of our spirit, soul, and body.

Deeper Light – Reflect + Respond

1. Read More

- Psalm 1:1–3
- Proverbs 4:20–23
- Joshua 1:8
- John 15:4–5
- 2 Corinthians 9:8

2. Journal Prompt

- What am I currently planting in the soil of my heart, God's truth or worldly influences?
- How does my view of "prosperity" align with God's Word rather than cultural ideas?
- Which area of my life- spirit, soul, or body- needs the most intentional investment right now?

3. Daily Declaration of Faith

"I prosper from the inside out. As my soul thrives in Christ, I walk in health, abundance, and blessing in every area of my life."

4. Live It Out

- Spend at least 10 minutes each day reading or meditating on Scripture this week.
- Replace one negative or unhelpful input (media, conversation, habit) with something that builds your spirit.
- Write down three specific ways you want to see God's prosperity grow in your life and pray over them daily.

Reflection

Guard Your Heart: Safeguarding Your Innocence

"Forgiveness is an act of the will, and the will can function regardless of the temperature of the heart."
Corrie Ten Boom

When Jesus said we must become like children again to enter the Kingdom of Heaven, He didn't mean we should act immature or speak in high-pitched voices. He was speaking of the posture of our hearts; that we must return to childlike innocence, trust, and humility. Children do not worry about bills or the future; they depend on their parents and rest securely in their love.

This is why the greatest assault in life is against your heart. The enemy will do everything in his power to damage it using pain, trauma, and betrayal because he knows that a heart tender before the Lord will manifest the supernatural. A childlike heart is where God moves through us most freely.

For the world's definition of an "adult" is simply a childlike heart that has resorted to cynicism.

On the outside, they may appear efficient and wise, planning and strategizing for the future, but on the inside, they've lost the wonder of surrender.

That's why we must guard our hearts above everything else.

Proverbs 4:23 AMPC *"Keep and guard your heart with all vigilance and above all that you guard, for out of it flow the springs of life."*

We must not allow the heart to grow hard from the things we've experienced. The enemy's strategy is often subtle and personal: he uses those closest to us to inflict the deepest wounds. Perhaps you've endured betrayal, manipulation, or even just a misinterpretation of someone's words. Regardless of the form, the result is the same— offense, and with it, the temptation to withhold forgiveness.

But harboring offense is dangerous. Consider the parable of the sower. The seed that landed on the pathway was never received; it simply sat on the surface and was eaten by birds. That pathway represents a hardened heart, one that can no longer receive God's Word.

So ask yourself: How are pathways created?

By people walking the same route over and over again.

A heart becomes a pathway when it's been trampled on repeatedly often by those you trusted most. Without forgiveness, those repeated offenses begin to layer and solidify, forming a hard shell around the heart. And in time, that heart forgets what childlike innocence ever felt like.

Proverbs 19:11 TPT *"An understanding person demonstrates patience, for mercy means holding your tongue. When you are insulted, be quick to forgive and forget it, for you are virtuous when you overlook an offense."*

This is why we must be attentive to the movements of our heart. We must forgive quickly especially when the wound is fresh. We must choose to walk in love, even when we are being ridiculed or harmed. We must bless those who curse us. One practical way I've learned to do this is to ask: What is their story? Have they been wounded?

People who have been hurt often hurt others. And when you see the pain behind their actions, it gives you the compassion you need to release them and yourself.

Forgiveness isn't just for them, it's for you. It keeps your heart soft and sensitive to God's voice. That's why we must confront everything that tries to harden our hearts. Bitterness must be dealt with fiercely. Unforgiveness must be uprooted quickly. Doing so will empower you to love deeply, forgive fiercely, and walk in unstoppable joy.

The world may call that kind of life weak or foolish, but don't waste your breath trying to defend yourself. God will lift you so high, His favor will speak louder than any insult ever could.

So love without fear.

Be bold in the face of pain.

Never relinquish your innocence by repaying evil for evil.

Imitate your Father, for He extends mercy to both the good and the evil.

Ephesians 5:1–2 *"Therefore be imitators of God as dear children. And walk in love, as Christ also has loved us and given Himself for us, an offering and a sacrifice to God for a sweet-smelling aroma."*

Matthew 5:44–45 *"But I say to you, love your enemies, bless those who curse you, do good to those who hate you, and pray for those who spitefully use you and persecute you, that you may be sons of your Father in heaven; for He makes His sun rise on the evil and on the good, and sends rain on the just and on the unjust."*

Light for the Path

A tender, childlike heart is where God's love and power flow most freely. Forgiveness protects your heart from becoming hardened, keeping you sensitive to His voice and full of His joy.

Deeper Light – Reflect + Respond

1. **Read More**

- Proverbs 4:23
- Matthew 18:1–4
- Colossians 3:12–14
- Luke 6:27–36
- 1 Peter 3:8–9

2. **Journal Prompt**

- Have I allowed repeated offenses to harden my heart in certain areas?
- Who do I need to forgive quickly so my heart remains soft toward God?
- What would it look like for me to walk in childlike trust and innocence again?

3. **Daily Declaration of Faith**

> *"My heart is tender before the Lord. I forgive quickly, walk in love, and guard my innocence, for out of my heart flow the springs of life."*

4. **Live It Out**

- Identify any offense you've been holding onto and release it in prayer today.
- When tempted to respond in anger, pause and choose mercy instead.
- Look for opportunities to bless someone who has hurt you, reflecting the mercy of your Father.

Reflection

Healing is in the Spirit: For Your Body

2 Peter 1:3–4 *"...as His divine power has given to us all things that pertain to life and godliness, through the knowledge of Him who called us by glory and virtue, by which have been given to us exceedingly great and precious promises, that through these you may be partakers of the divine nature, having escaped the corruption that is in the world through lust."*

Everything we need for life has already been provided by our Father. The challenge for most believers is not in getting what they need, but in learning how to release what they already have. What we've been given is spiritual in nature—spiritual realities that often stand in direct contradiction to the natural realm.

Philemon 1:6 *"...that the sharing of your faith may become effective by the acknowledgment of every good thing which is in you in Christ Jesus."*

What we need is already within us in the Spirit. But if we live only by the natural, we will find it impossible to walk in the supernatural. Releasing what is in the Spirit requires us to be spiritually minded, exalting the truth of the Spirit above our natural senses.

Romans 8:5–6 *"For those who live according to the flesh set their minds on the things of the flesh, but those who live according to the Spirit, the things of the Spirit. For to be carnally minded is death, but to be spiritually minded is life and peace."*

Take supernatural healing, for example. Though Jesus told us that we would do the same works He did (**John 14:12**), many believers cling to traditions that say healing has passed away. They believe this not because Scripture teaches it, but because they elevate their experiences above the Word of God. Rather than asking where they might be missing it, they craft doctrines that justify their lack of power. And Jesus made it clear how much He opposes such teaching:

Matthew 15:9 *"'And in vain they worship Me, teaching as doctrines the commandments of men.'"*

But Scripture teaches that we can walk in divine healing! Consider this powerful truth:

Romans 8:10–11 *"And if Christ is in you, the body is dead because of sin, but the Spirit is life because of righteousness. But if the Spirit of Him who raised Jesus from the dead dwells in you, He who raised Christ from the dead will also give life to your mortal bodies through His Spirit who dwells in you."*

Though death still lingers in our flesh since our physical bodies haven't yet been redeemed, life abounds in our spirit because we are united with Christ (**1 Corinthians 6:17**). Remember, it is the spirit that gives life to the body (**John 6:63; James 2:26**). Since resurrection life lives in our spirit, it can overflow into our physical bodies. If healing is in my spirit, then sickness cannot stay in my body. My body is the temple of the living God, and His glory pushes out all sickness and disease. His Spirit radiates from within spilling into my soul and flesh. Life and death cannot cohabitate; life overcomes death and drives it out.

Romans 8:2 *"For the law of the Spirit of life in Christ Jesus has made me free from the law of sin and death."*

Where Life is, death must pass over.

Exodus 12:13 *"Now the blood shall be a sign for you on the houses where you are. And when I see the blood, I will pass over you; and the plague shall not be on you to destroy you when I strike the land of Egypt."*

The blood of Jesus has cleansed us from all unrighteousness and made us new. In the Spirit, the blood has been applied, and therefore death has no right to us. Our bodies are temples of the glory of God and where His glory resides, the curse cannot.

So how do we release this healing power from our spirit into the natural? The answer is simple: we speak the Word.

Proverbs 18:20–21 *"A man's stomach shall be satisfied from the fruit of his mouth; From the produce of his lips he shall be filled. Death and life are in the power of the tongue, And those who love it will eat its fruit."*

Find the scripture that promises healing and speak only that Word not your symptoms. Sickness may scream for your attention, but you must resist and keep your eyes on God's promises. Just as Abraham did not consider his own body though it was as good as dead, but believed only what God had said (**Romans 4:19**), so must we. He refused to be moved by what he saw, and chose instead to believe the Word, trusting that God's truth was higher than natural facts. This is what it means to:

2 Corinthians 5:7 *"...walk by faith, not by sight."*

We live by what God says not by what we feel, see, or experience in the natural (**Deuteronomy 8:3**). So keep speaking the Word of God. Hold fast your confession (**Hebrews 10:23**), and thank Him in advance for the manifestation (**Philippians 4:6**). If God cannot lie (**Hebrews 6:18**), then our persistent declaration of His Word proves we believe Him over what we see or feel.

And don't forget His eternal promise:

Exodus 15:26 *"...If you diligently heed the voice of the LORD your God and do what is right in His sight, give ear to His commandments and keep all His statutes, I will put none of the diseases on you which I have brought on the Egyptians. For **I am** the LORD who heals you."*

"I Am" signifies unchanging identity. God is and always will be our Healer. He has provided healing for every child of God united to Christ. So loose your tongue and declare the healing that already belongs to you! When you speak His Word, heaven responds.

Jeremiah 1:12 *"Then the LORD said to me, 'You have seen well, for I am ready to perform My word.'"*

Light for the Path

Healing is already in your spirit because the Spirit of Christ lives in you. As you speak God's Word in faith, that life flows from your spirit into your body, driving out sickness and manifesting His promises.

Deeper Light – Reflect + Respond

1. Read More

- Romans 8:10–11
- 1 Peter 2:24
- Proverbs 4:20–22
- Matthew 8:16–17
- Mark 11:22–25

2. Journal Prompt

- Do I believe that God has already placed healing within my spirit?
- What natural symptoms or circumstances have I been exalting above God's Word?
- How can I become more consistent in speaking only God's promises over my body?

3. Daily Declaration of Faith

"The Spirit of life in Christ lives in me. His resurrection power gives life to my body, drives out sickness, and keeps me whole. My body is His temple, and His glory makes me strong."

4. **Live It Out**

- Choose one healing scripture and declare it daily over your body.
- Resist the urge to speak about symptoms; replace them with faith-filled words from God's Word.
- Spend time praising God each day for the healing that is already yours in the Spirit.

Reflection

_____

_____

_____

_____

_____

_____

_____

_____

_____

_____

_____

_____

_____

_____

_____

_____

_____

_____

_____

Week 16

Healing is In Your Spirit: For Your Heart

Proverbs 20:27 KJV *"The spirit of man is the candle of the LORD, Searching all the inward parts of the belly."*

Candles must be lit in order to give light. Yet every human being born into this world is spiritually dead, their candle unlit. Until salvation comes, the human spirit remains dormant, unable to shine. Can a person navigate a darkened room with an unlit candle? Of course not—they will stumble, unable to see what lies before them.

Proverbs 4:19 NLT *"But the way of the wicked is like total darkness. They have no idea what they are stumbling over."*

Jesus is the source of that Light. His desire is that all would receive it. He came to bring Light so that no one would remain in darkness, deprived of the illumination of God's truth about Him and about themselves.

John 1:4 *"In Him was life, and the life was the light of men."*

Luke 1:79 *"To give light to those who sit in darkness and the shadow of death, To guide our feet into the way of peace."*

But when a person turns to the Lord for salvation—Hallelujah!—their spirit is born again. Their candle is relit!

Luke 8:16–17 *"No one, when he has lit a lamp, covers it with a vessel or puts it under a bed, but sets it on a lampstand, that those who enter may see the light. For nothing is secret that will not be revealed, nor anything hidden that will not be known and come to light."*

This passage and the opening verse from Proverbs reveal the purpose of a relit candle in Christ: to expose what was once hidden in darkness. And where are those hidden things? In your "belly."

Proverbs 20:27 KJV *"The spirit of man is the candle of the LORD, Searching all the inward parts of the **belly**."*

What does the "belly" refer to? It speaks to the deep places of the human soul. Remember, the purpose of faith—the supernatural power that resides in your spirit—is to save your soul. In other words, the goal of this supernatural faith is to bring your soul into alignment with your spirit, which has been made new in Christ.

Your soul carries the pain, trauma, shame, unforgiveness, and wounds accumulated before salvation. It is faith that drives those things out and cleanses your inner life. This is why soul transformation is impossible for the person who has not been born again. It's like trying to navigate a dark room with an unlit candle.

But when your spirit is reborn, when that candle is finally lit, you now carry the light of divine illumination. And by that light, you can discern the thoughts, emotions, and memories within your soul that do not align with your new identity in Christ. Hallelujah!

This is why we can boldly declare, along with all believers:

2 Peter 1:3 *"As His divine power has given to us all things that pertain to life and godliness, through the knowledge of Him who called us by glory and virtue."*

So don't shrink back from inner pain. Instead, face it knowing that you already carry within your spirit the power to bring healing and wholeness to your heart. Your identity is no longer built around the defense mechanisms you developed to protect your wounds. You can now let go of the pseudo-self, the false version of you that formed to hide the hurt.

Like Adam hiding from the Lord in the garden, you can now come out of hiding, confident that the person you once were in sin is not the person you are in Christ. You are one with Him, and you now have the power and authority to serve eviction notices to every trace of pain that has tried to hold you captive or paralyze your purpose.

Push forward. You were made for victory. You were destined for glory.

Romans 8:37 *"Yet in all these things we are more than conquerors through Him who loved us."*

Light for the Path

When your spirit is born again, the light of Christ exposes what is hidden in your soul so it can be healed. The same power that raised Jesus from the dead now works within you to bring freedom, restoration, and victory.

Deeper Light – Reflect + Respond

1. Read More

- John 8:12
- Philippians 4:13
- Ephesians 1:17–19
- 1 John 4:4, 5:4
- Zechariah 4:6

2. Journal Prompt

- What wounds, memories, or thought patterns still linger in the "deep places" of my soul?
- How can I invite the light of Christ to search and heal those areas?
- What false identities or defense mechanisms have I built to protect myself, and am I ready to release them?

3. Daily Declaration of Faith

"My spirit is alive in Christ, and His light searches the deep places of my heart. By faith, I cast out every wound, lie, and fear, and I walk in

wholeness. I am more than a conqueror, healed and made new through Jesus."

4. **Live It Out**

- Spend quiet time inviting the Holy Spirit to reveal any hidden wounds or lies in your heart.
- Write down one area you sense He wants to heal and find Scripture to speak over it daily.
- Take a bold step to walk in your new identity; do something you've avoided because of past pain.

Reflection

_____

_____

_____

_____

_____

_____

_____

_____

_____

_____

_____

_____

_____

_____

Healing the Heart: The Purpose of Faith

Matthew 13:15 *'For the hearts of this people have grown dull. Their ears are hard of hearing, and their eyes they have closed, Lest they should see with their eyes and hear with their ears, Lest they should understand with their hearts and turn, So that I should heal them."*

Notice that when we open our eyes (which is turning our mind inwards to deal with the issues we see manifesting in our hearts), then healing can come. This was the very purpose for which Jesus came.

Luke 4:18 *"The Spirit of the Lord is upon Me, Because He has anointed Me To preach the gospel to the poor; He has sent Me to* **heal the brokenhearted**, *To proclaim liberty to the captives And recovery of sight to the blind, To set at liberty those who are oppressed;"*

It is not faith to only speak the word, and yet ignore the doubt that festers in your heart. You must go through a process where you cleanse your heart so that it is pure and in agreement with the words you speak.

Romans 10:8 *'But what does it say? "The word is near you, in your mouth* **and** *in your heart" (that is, the word of faith which we preach)."*

Notice that the "word of faith" refers not only to the words we speak, but also to when our hearts are in alignment with those words. Those two criteria must be fulfilled before the word of God is manifested in our lives with power and authority.

You cannot heal your heart when you are walking in pride. Pride refuses to see character flaws and thus cannot receive inner healing. Healing of the heart can only be appropriated through humility.

I Peter 5:6-7 *"Therefore humble yourselves under the mighty hand of God, that He may exalt you in due time, casting all your care upon Him, for He cares for you."*

When we cast all our distracting concerns upon Christ and nullify their power over our souls through the strength of His Spirit within us, healing follows.

I John 2:27 *"But the anointing which you have received from Him abides in you, and you do not need that anyone teach you; but as the same anointing teaches you concerning all things, and is true, and is not a lie, and just as it has taught you, you will abide in Him."*

It is the power of the Spirit within us to teach us and leads us into healing.

Our heart—what is it, really? I believe it to be the central part of our soul, that part of us from which all our passions issue forth from. It inspires our thoughts and shapes a disposition within us that creates an affinity for certain things and ways of living. Think of this; our physical heart is the central part of our body. Out of it issues forth all the body needs to live. If the heart is bad, the whole body will suffer. This helps us understand the warning given in the proverb;

Proverbs 4:23 *"Keep your heart with all diligence, For out of it spring the issues of life."*

Our heart is the central part of our soul, that place from which all our desires originate. We must guard our heart, for the enemy will seek to sow seeds of weeds and thistles (lies) that prevent the word of God from coming to fruition in our lives. When our hearts are filled with unforgiveness, doubt, bitterness, rage, hatred, and similar things, they hinder the Word of God from manifesting in our lives. We may speak the Word with our mouths, but our hearts are not convinced. In order to see the power flow, we must cleanse our hearts. That's right! This is not Gods job, but our own, for if we have believed the lies of the enemy, it is our responsibility to uproot those weeds, not His. That's why, when I recently noticed pain rising from my heart over things I had agreed to, I heard the Lord distinctly say, "I did not do this—this is something **YOU** must deal with. I allowed it in; therefore, it's my responsibility to kick it out.

James 4:7-10 *"Therefore submit to God. Resist the devil and he will flee from you. Draw near to God and He will draw near to you. Cleanse your hands, you sinners; and purify your hearts, you double-minded. Lament and mourn and weep! Let your laughter be turned to mourning and your joy to gloom. Humble yourselves in the sight of the Lord, and He will lift you up."*

Notice it says, **YOU** clean your hands and **YOU** purify your hearts. That is our job.

II Timothy 2:20-21 *"But in a great house there are not only vessels of gold and silver, but also of wood and clay, some for honor and some for dishonor. Therefore, if anyone cleanses himself from the latter, he will be a vessel for honor, sanctified and useful for the Master, prepared for every good work."*

If anyone **CLEANSES HIMSELF**! It is our responsibility to cast down any thoughts in our hearts that are not in alignment with the Word. Therefore, we must know the Word and use it to cleanse and guard our hearts.

II Corinthians 10:3-5 *"For though we walk in the flesh, we do not war according to the flesh. For the weapons of our warfare are not carnal but mighty in God for pulling down strongholds, casting down arguments and every high thing that exalts itself against the knowledge of God, bringing every thought into captivity to the obedience of Christ,"*

Light for the Path

Faith has been deposited into your spirit to bring healing to your heart. It is your responsibility to steward that heart well. By faith, guard it diligently, and refuse to let weeds take root where God's seed has been planted.

Deeper Light – Reflect + Respond

1. Read More

- Matthew 5:8
- Ezekiel 36:26–27
- Hebrews 10:22
- Psalm 51:10–12
- James 1:21–25

2. Journal Prompt

- What thoughts, lies, or heart attitudes are out of alignment with God's Word in my life?
- Have I been waiting for God to do something in my heart that He has already given me the authority to address?
- How can I actively "pull up the weeds" that choke the truth in my heart?

3. Daily Declaration of Faith

"I guard my heart and keep it pure. I resist the devil and he flees. I am a vessel of honor, cleansed by the Word, filled with faith, and strengthened by the Spirit. Healing and wholeness flow in me through Christ."

4. Live It Out

- Take time today to ask the Holy Spirit to reveal any areas of your heart that may need cleansing.
- Find Scripture that speaks truth into that area and meditate on it daily.
- Replace negative inner dialogue with declarations of God's promises.

Reflection

Week 18

CALLED OUT

Genesis 12:1 (NLT) *"The Lord had said to Abram, "Leave your native country, your relatives, and your father's family, and go to the land that I will show you."*

Why does God call us out?

Why does He lead us out of our comfort zones, away from our relatives, and beyond everything familiar and dependable?

Jesus answered this clearly in **Luke 14:26 (ERV)**:

"If you come to me but will not leave your family, you cannot be my follower. You must love me more than your father, mother, wife, children, brothers, and sisters— even more than your own life!"

When God says, *"Leave,"* our natural response is often, *"But why?"* *"Can't I grow right where I am?"*

The answer is simple: No. Because comfort breeds complacency.

Jesus never said, "Stay." His command was clear:

Mark 16:15 (NLT) *"**Go** into all the world and preach the Good News to everyone."*

If we want to grow in Christ and become more like Him, we must reject a lifestyle built on ease. Abram was seventy-five years old when God called him to leave everything familiar and step into obedience. His age didn't exempt him, and neither does ours. It's never too late to respond to God's call.

Growth is always found in change, and in immediate obedience.

According to Jesus, this obedience may cost us everything. Yet one of the most beautiful truths about our Savior is this: He never calls us to difficult things without attaching a promise to them.

Mark 10:28-30 (NLT) *"Then Peter began to speak up. "We've given up everything to follow you," he said. "Yes," Jesus replied, "and I assure you that everyone who has given up house or brothers or sisters or mother or father or children or property, for my sake and for the Good News, will receive now in return a hundred times as many houses, brothers, sisters, mothers, children, and property—along with persecution. And in the world to come that person will have eternal life."*

Even in surrender, God's heart is redemption and restoration. He never asks us to give up someone or something without the intention of returning it multiplied.

Job 42:10 (NLT) *"When Job prayed for his friends, the Lord restored his fortunes. In fact, the Lord gave him twice as much as before!"* (Read verses 10–13 to see how abundantly the Lord blessed him.)

There is growth in leaving what you know, for the sake of knowing the One who knows you. That's why He called Abram out, and that's why He still calls us out today.

Growth in Christ unlocks the blessings of the Lord.

Genesis 12:2–3 (NLT) *"I will make you into a great nation. I will bless you and make you famous, and you will be a blessing to others. I will bless those who bless you and curse those who treat you with contempt. All the families on earth will be blessed through you."*

We cannot pour out what we haven't first received. Like Abraham, the blessings that follow our obedience won't just be for us, they will overflow into generations after us.

Obedience came first. Then came the blessing.

Let's stop expecting the latter without walking in the former.

Light for the Path

God calls us out of comfort so that He can call us into destiny. Growth never comes from staying where it's safe and familiar; it comes from trusting His voice above every other and stepping into obedience.

Deeper Light – Reflect + Respond

1. **Read More**

- Genesis 12:1–4
- Luke 14:26–27
- Mark 10:28–30
- Matthew 16:25
- Hebrews 11:8–10

2. **Journal Prompt**

- What is God asking me to leave behind in this season?
- Am I delaying obedience because I'm waiting for comfort or clarity?
- How might my obedience today impact others in the future?

3. **Daily Declaration of Faith**

"I will not cling to comfort or fear the unknown. I follow where the Lord leads, and His blessings flow through my obedience. I am called out, set apart, and positioned for greater things in Christ."

4. Live It Out

- Identify one step of obedience God is calling you to take and commit to act on it this week.
- Share with a trusted believer what God is leading you to do, so they can encourage and pray with you.
- Keep a record of how God provides and fulfills His promises along the way.

Reflection

_____

_____

_____

_____

_____

_____

_____

_____

_____

_____

_____

_____

_____

_____

_____

_____

_____

_____

_____

_____

Maturing in Christ

There are steps we must take in order to mature in Christ. Maturity doesn't "just happen." One of the most important things to understand about spiritual maturity is that, according to the Bible, it is not optional; it is expected!

We see this truth clearly in the parable of the talents in **Matthew 25:14–30**. The Master (God) is only pleased with the two servants whose talents matured and multiplied. He specifically praises them, saying:

"Well done, my good and faithful servant. You have been faithful in handling this small amount, so now I will give you many more responsibilities. Let's celebrate together!"

However, the servant who did nothing with what he was given, who neither matured nor multiplied, was met with a very different response:

Matthew 25:26–27 NLT *"You wicked and lazy servant! If you knew I harvested crops I didn't plant and gathered crops I didn't cultivate, why didn't you deposit my money in the bank? At least I could have gotten some interest on it"*

This parable proves a vital principle: God desires His children to mature, to multiply, and to increase. He is not content with us staying stagnant and unfruitful. In fact, He refers to unfaithful and idle servants as **"wicked and lazy."**

I don't know about you, but I do not want to be called a wicked and lazy servant of the Lord. I want to be known as a good and faithful servant; someone my Lord and Savior can trust with whatever He places in my hands, whether spiritual or physical.

Step 1: **Move Beyond the Basics**

The first step to spiritual maturity is to stop laying the same spiritual foundation over and over again. What good is it to continually relearn what we've already been taught? Even in grade school, once you've mastered one level, you move on. So why do we treat biblical principles any differently?

Hebrews 6:1 says:

> *"Therefore, leaving the discussion of the elementary principles of Christ, let us go on to perfection, not laying again the foundation of repentance from dead works and of faith toward God."*

The next verse, **Hebrews 6:2**, lists these foundational teachings: **repentance, faith in God, baptisms, laying on of hands, resurrection of the dead, and eternal judgment**. The writer of Hebrews urges believers not to remain stuck in the basics, such as repentance from dead works, but to build upon them and move toward spiritual maturity.

As **1 Corinthians 3:2** puts it, we are to move from milk to solid food in our faith.

Step 2: **Be Planted in a Church Community**

The next step in spiritual growth is to be part of a church and a community that encourages and facilitates maturity.

Hebrews 10:25 (NLT) reminds us:

> *"And let us not neglect our meeting together, as some people do, but encourage one another, especially now that the day of his return is drawing near."*

Many believers who struggle to grow are those who lack commitment to a church body. They drift in and out without accountability or connection. But Scripture shows us the power of community:

James 5:16 (NLT) says:

"Confess your sins to each other and pray for each other so that you may be healed. The earnest prayer of a righteous person has great power and produces wonderful results."

God desires a community of believers marked by transparency, prayer, and accountability; this is how we grow.

Step 3: **Be Rooted in the Word**

To mature in Christ, we must be rooted in the Word of God. The seeds planted in the soil of your heart need the daily washing of the Word to grow. The more Scripture you take in, the more transformation you will see.

Romans 12:2 (MSG) says:

"Don't become so well-adjusted to your culture that you fit into it without even thinking. Instead, fix your attention on God. You'll be changed from the inside out… God brings the best out of you, develops well-formed maturity in you."

There is no spiritual maturity without the renewing of your mind by the Word of God. If you've found yourself in a place of complacency, you can make the choice today to dive into Scripture; allow it to cleanse you, renew your mind, and reshape your life.

The Bible also warns us about the dangers of immaturity and indifference:

Hebrews 6:11–12 (NLT) says:

"Our great desire is that you will keep on loving others as long as life lasts, in order to make certain that what you hope for will come true. Then you will not become spiritually dull and indifferent. Instead, you will follow the example of those who are going to inherit God's promises because of their faith and endurance."

This is a call to active, enduring faith, not passive belief. Don't neglect what God has placed in you. Nurture it!

Light for the Path

Spiritual maturity requires intentional growth, moving beyond the basics, being planted in community, and being rooted in God's Word, so that we multiply what He has entrusted to us.

Deeper Light – Reflect + Respond

1. Read More

- Matthew 25:14–30
- Hebrews 6:1–2
- Hebrews 10:23-25
- Romans 12:2
- Hebrews 6:11–12

2. Journal Prompt

- Which area of my walk with God; foundations, community, or time in the Word, needs the most attention right now?
- Am I faithfully multiplying what God has entrusted to me, or am I stagnant?
- How can I take one step forward in my spiritual growth this week?

3. Daily Declaration of Faith

"I am a faithful servant of Christ. I move beyond spiritual basics, I am rooted in His Word, and I grow in community. By His Spirit, I am maturing, multiplying, and increasing in every good work."

4. **Live It Out**

- Identify one spiritual discipline to deepen, whether prayer, Bible study, or fellowship, and commit to it this week.
- Declare this word over your life; "I will allow the Word of God to renew my mind by reading it daily and allowing it to change me from the inside out, growing and maturing in my faith in Him." (Romans 12:2)
- Keep a journal of how God grows your faith as you apply His Word daily.

Reflection

_____

_____

_____

_____

_____

_____

_____

_____

_____

_____

_____

_____

_____

_____

_____

_____

_____

_____

Week 20

BLANK CANVAS

Hebrews 11:8 (TPT) *"Faith motivated Abraham to obey God's call and leave the familiar to discover the territory he was destined to inherit from God. So he left with only a promise and without even knowing ahead of time where he was going, Abraham stepped out in faith."*

Humility is choosing to leave the canvas of your life blank and allowing God to fill it with the beauty of His promises.

As **James 4:10** reminds us, *"Humble yourselves before the Lord, and He will lift you up in honor."*

Abraham's faith is a powerful example of this truth. He did not obsess over the details of the promise; **instead**, he focused on the Promiser. He obeyed immediately, trusting in God's character and in His ability to fulfill all that He had spoken.

Many believers today receive a promise from God, but then rush to paint their own picture of how it will be fulfilled; filling the canvas with personal ideas, timelines, and expectations. Yet God says, "Leave it blank, and let Me lead you by faith, just as I did with Abraham."

Romans 8:14 (NLT) *"For all who are led by the Spirit of God are children of God."*

When we try to force God's vision to fit our own, we step out of humility and begin designing from a place of pride. Scripture warns us:

Proverbs 18:12 *"Before destruction the heart of a man is haughty, and before honor is humility."*

This "destruction" does not always arrive as a sudden catastrophe. It can come subtly, as severed expectations, lingering discouragement, or even a distorted view of God's Word. Over time, we stop expecting to see the words of Jesus manifest in our lives. We settle. We grow spiritually complacent.

But Jesus said:

John 14:12 (NLT) *"I tell you the truth, anyone who believes in Me will do the same works I have done, and even greater works, because I am going to be with the Father."*

And again:

Mark 16:17–18 (NLT) *"These miraculous signs will accompany those who believe: They will cast out demons in My name, and they will speak in new languages. They will be able to handle snakes with safety, and if they drink anything poisonous, it won't hurt them. They will be able to place their hands on the sick, and they will be healed."*

There is no power in a complacent Christian life. Power is found in surrender, in becoming a new creation in Christ. A blank canvas.

2 Corinthians 5:17 *"Therefore, if anyone is in Christ, he is a new creation; old things have passed away; behold, all things have become new."*

The Lord's power and glory follow the humble. Leave your canvas blank, and watch Him create a masterpiece.

Ephesians 2:10 (NLT) *"For we are God's masterpiece. He has created us anew in Christ Jesus, so we can do the good things he planned for us long ago."*

Light for the Path

True humility is leaving the canvas of your life blank and trusting God to paint it with His promises, just as Abraham did when he stepped out in faith without knowing the way.

Deeper Light – Reflect + Respond

1. Read More

- Hebrews 11:8–10
- Proverbs 18:12
- Romans 8:14–17
- 2 Corinthians 5:17
- Ephesians 2:10

2. Journal Prompt

- In what areas of my life am I still trying to control the "painting," rather than leaving the canvas blank for God?
- How has pride or impatience shaped my expectations of God's promises?
- What does becoming God's masterpiece mean for how I live today?

3. Daily Declaration of Faith

> *"By faith I leave the canvas of my life in God's hands. He fills it with His promises, and I trust His plan for me."*

4. Live It Out

- Identify one area this week where you will intentionally surrender control to God.
- Replace one anxious or pride-filled thought with a truth from Scripture (e.g., 2 Corinthians 5:17; Ephesians 2:10).
- Declare over your life; I will meditate on Your Word day and night, and You will make my way prosperous and cause me to succeed in ALL I do!

Reflection

RELY ON JESUS

Philippians 3:3 (NLT) *"For we who worship by the Spirit of God are the ones who are truly circumcised. We rely on what Christ Jesus has done for us. We put no confidence in human effort."*

According to Paul, circumcision is no longer about the physical act; it is now a matter of the heart, made possible through Jesus. This is incredibly good news for all of us living under the new covenant of Christ.

We no longer have to rely on our own strength. Instead, we now get to fully depend on what Jesus has already accomplished.

Paul tells the Philippians that if anyone had a reason to boast about their accomplishments, he would be at the top of the list (**Philippians 3:6**). But as he continues, he reveals how he now views all of his former achievements:

Philippians 3:7 (MSG) *"I once thought these things were valuable, but now I consider them worthless because of what Christ has done."*

"The very credentials these people are waving around as something special, I'm tearing up and throwing out with the trash, along with everything else I used to take credit for. And why? Because of Christ."

Paul once took great pride in all he had accomplished, until he encountered Jesus. That moment redefined everything. This is the heart of salvation: being rescued from striving, from trying to save ourselves, and from the grip of sin, death, and hell.

In Christ, we stop measuring our worth by what we've done (good or bad) and begin resting in what Jesus has done.

That is a powerful shift!

Compared to the finished work of the cross, anything we've done in our own strength holds no value.

Scripture is clear: our best attempts at righteousness, apart from Christ, amount to nothing.

Isaiah 64:6 (NLT) *"We are all infected and impure with sin. When we display our righteous deeds, they are nothing but filthy rags. Like autumn leaves, we wither and fall, and our sins sweep us away like the wind."*

So why do we keep striving? Why do we treat co-laboring with Christ as if it means, *"I'll make the plan, You just bless it and make it work"*?

Recently, after a church service, the Lord reminded me that none of the promises He's given me will come to pass through human effort. They will only be fulfilled by listening to Him and walking in obedience. It really is that simple, but we often complicate it with flesh-driven striving.

God calls us to produce fruit that remains, but fruit like that can't come from human effort; it only comes through the One who chose us, appointed us, and works through us.

John 15:16 (NLT) *"You didn't choose me. I chose you. I appointed you to go and produce lasting fruit, so that the Father will give you whatever you ask for, using my name."*

Fruit produced in our own strength won't last. Only what is born through Jesus endures. That's the only kind of fruit worth pursuing. Everything else is garbage.

Righteousness comes through faith in Christ, nothing else.

Philippians 3:8–9 (NLT) *"Yes, everything else is worthless when compared with the infinite value of knowing Christ Jesus my Lord. For his sake I have discarded everything else, counting it all as garbage, so that I could gain Christ and become one with him. I no longer count on my own righteousness through obeying* *the law; rather, I become righteous through faith in Christ. For God's way of making us right with himself depends on faith."*

To those who feel like they have to clean themselves up before coming to Christ, Scripture says otherwise. Righteousness doesn't come by effort; it comes by faith. It starts by coming to Him just as you are. That's where transformation begins. He alone has the power to change your life.

Light for the Path

Righteousness and lasting fruit don't come from our effort but from relying fully on what Christ has already accomplished.

Deeper Light – Reflect + Respond

1. Read More

- Philippians 3:3–9
- John 15:1–8, 16
- Isaiah 64:6
- Romans 3:21–26
- Galatians 2:20, 3:10

2. Journal Prompt

- In what areas of my life am I still relying on my own strength instead of Jesus?
- How do I measure my worth; by what I've done, or by what Christ has done for me?
- What would it look like for me to fully rest in Jesus' finished work?

3. Daily Declaration of Faith

"I put no confidence in my own effort. My righteousness comes through faith in Christ alone."

4. **Live It Out**

- This week, replace one self-reliant thought ("I must make this work") with a truth from Scripture ("It is Christ who works in me," Phil. 2:13).
- Identify one area where you've been striving in your own effort, then pause, surrender it to Jesus in prayer, and ask Him for direction.
- Declare over your life; "From now on, I regard my human efforts as garbage compared to what Jesus did for me. I choose to rely on what He did and not on what I can do."

Reflection

_____

_____

_____

_____

_____

_____

_____

_____

_____

_____

_____

_____

_____

_____

_____

_____

_____

_____

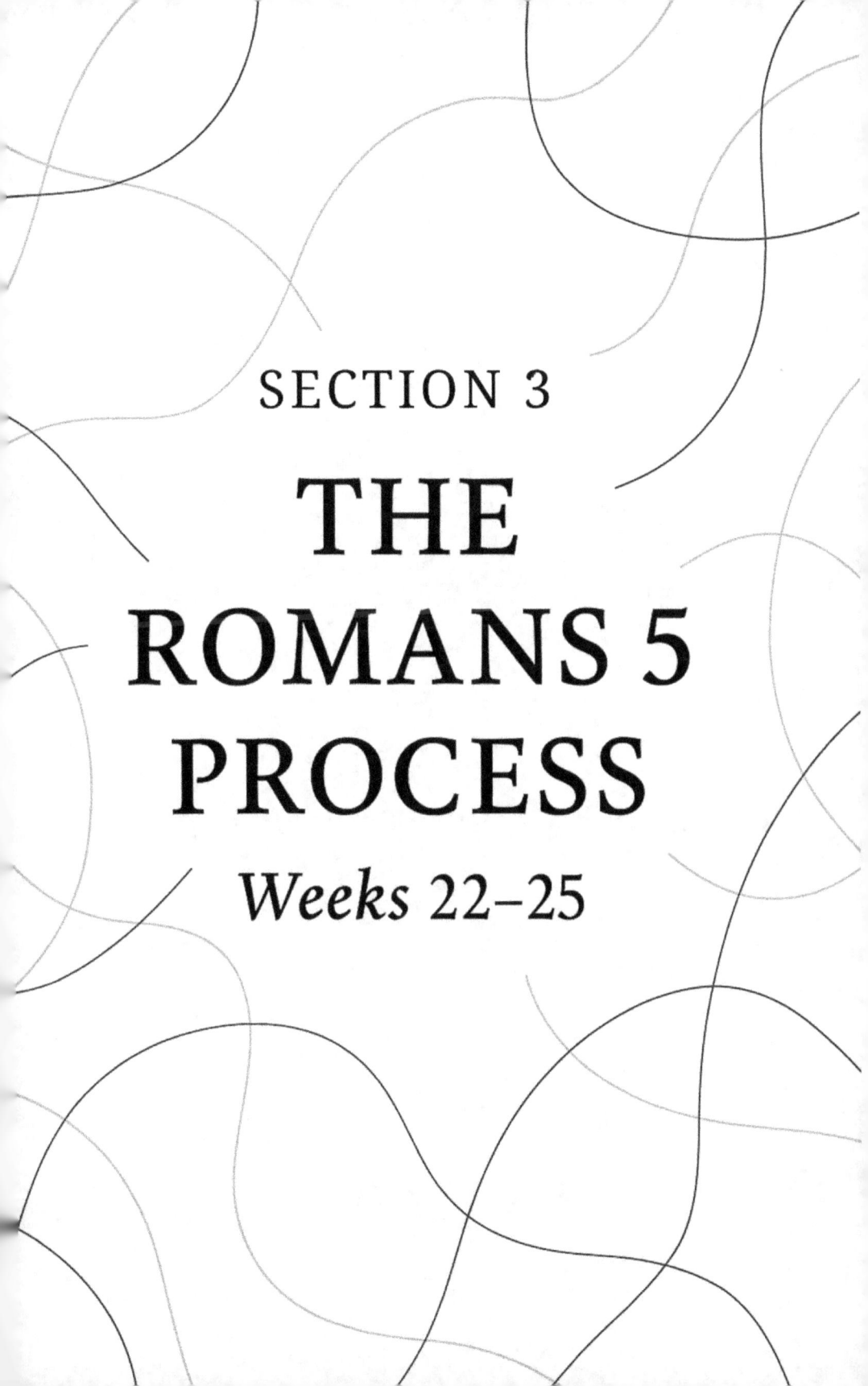

SECTION 3

THE
ROMANS 5
PROCESS

Weeks 22–25

Week 22

Part 1: Perseverance

Romans 5:3–5 *"And not only that, but we also glory in tribulations, knowing that tribulation produces perseverance; and perseverance, character; and character, hope. Now hope does not disappoint, because the love of God has been poured out in our hearts by the Holy Spirit who was given to us."*

Tribulations or pressures in the life of a believer serve a specific and powerful purpose. However, before we explore that, we must establish something foundational: God is never the author of our suffering. It is the enemy who comes to steal, kill, and destroy. Jesus, by contrast, came so that we might not only have life, but have it more abundantly (**John 10:10**).

This abundant life is the deepest longing of the human soul: to be reconnected to Life Himself in such a divine and intimate way that it produces an experience of joy beyond words (**1 Peter 1:8**). Yet the path to that life is one marked by suffering and warfare, not because God brings it, but because the enemy of our soul violently opposes us, seeking to block us from experiencing what he has forever lost.

So, dear child of God, settle it firmly in your heart: God is always good. There is no deception in Him (**James 1:16–17; 1 John 1:5**). By His very nature, He cannot lure anyone deceptively into a harmful situation only to ensnare them in it. To suggest that God would do such a thing is not only erroneous, but borders on blasphemy. Every good and perfect gift comes from God, never evil. The trouble that enters our lives is the work of the enemy, not the hand of our loving Father.

We must also confront a common but unspoken belief prevalent in much of the Western church: that becoming a child of God means smooth sailing until we peacefully pass into eternity. This is far from the truth. We are living in a war zone. Although the ultimate battle has already been won by Christ, we dwell among rebellious spiritual forces who will not bow unless they are forced to. As a result, we will be targets of the enemy and his schemes.

Jesus Himself warned us plainly:

> **John 16:33** *"These things I have spoken to you, that in Me you may have peace. In the world you will have tribulation; but be of good cheer, I have overcome the world."*

We experience peace when we step into our new identity in Christ where the power to overcome is already available to us. Though the enemy may bring tribulations, God uses those very trials to teach us how to walk more fully in who we are in Him. Let this powerful truth settle deeply in your heart and become something you continually feed on: because you are in Christ, you are already an overcomer! You possess all the power and resources you need to defeat every attack that comes against you.

We're not fighting to get something—No! We are fighting to enforce what already belongs to us in Christ. We're not victims trying to gain victory; we're victors commanding the enemy to back off what's already ours. The Word declares that we are more than conquerors (**Romans 8:37**), and when we stand in faith, we cannot be overcome (**1 John 5:4**)!

Notice that the scripture says, "we glory in tribulations." But what does it mean to glory in tribulation? It means declaring the end from the beginning. A person who carries this revelation will activate their faith by speaking words of faith when trouble comes knocking at their door. They'll say things like, *"Yes, the enemy may be trying to throw this on me, but thank God He has already promised me deliverance!"* This is the mindset of champions and overcomers: they refuse to let the trial define the outcome. Instead, they declare the outcome with confidence and unwavering faith, no matter what comes because they know the victory is already theirs in Christ!

Notice it also states, "Tribulation produces perseverance." The Greek word for produces means **"to work out, to effect, to bring forth as a result**." When we endure tribulations with God, something is being worked out of us and something else is being formed in us— namely, perseverance.

Perseverance is not passive. It's not about simply enduring while getting pummeled. The word means **"patient endurance**," or **"adhering steadfastly to an object**." This definition becomes even more revealing when we distinguish between belief and faith.

Faith is actually a fruit of the Spirit:

Galatians 5:22 *"But the fruit of the Spirit is…faith…"*

If faith is a fruit of the Spirit, and faith is the only thing that pleases God (**Hebrews 11:6**), then how do we operate in faith? The answer is found in learning to *"walk in step with the Spirit"* (**Galatians 5:16–17**). When you walk in step with the Spirit, you are simultaneously crucifying the flesh, for *"the flesh lusts against the Spirit, and the Spirit against the flesh."* In this way, crucifying the flesh becomes the very key that empowers you to walk in the power of faith (**Galatians 5:24**). This is where perseverance comes in—it acts as the refining flame that burns away the flesh along with its passions and lusts.

Belief and faith are not the same. Belief can be shallow, held only while it's beneficial. The moment it seems inconvenient or painful, many let it go. This is why the shallow hearted fall away when tribulation comes for the Word's sake (see **Matthew 13:21; Mark 4:17; Luke 8:13**). In contrast, faith clings to the promise of God even when that promise seems distant or ineffective.

Faith, born of the Spirit, holds fast to our confession (**Hebrews 10:23**) even in seasons when God feels far away. In doing so, we crucify the flesh, its instinctive reactions, fears, and doubts and allow the Spirit to rise.

So in trials, when perseverance is worked in us, what is truly happening is the burning away of what is fleshly, revealing what is eternal: the Spirit. And from that refining comes character.

Light for the Path

Trials are not sent by God, but He uses them to form perseverance in us, burning away the flesh and strengthening Spirit-born faith that clings to His promises.

Deeper Light – Reflect + Respond

1. Read More

- Romans 5:3–5
- John 16:33
- Galatians 5:16–24
- Hebrews 10:23
- 1 John 5:4

2. Journal Prompt

- How do I usually respond when tribulation comes—by fear and striving, or by declaring God's promise?
- Where is God calling me to move from shallow belief into Spirit-born faith?
- What "fleshly reactions" do I need to crucify so perseverance can grow in me?

3. Daily Declaration of Faith

"I speak the end from the beginning like my Father does; I have the victory! And my relentless pursuit of the Lord produces perseverance in me. I am an overcomer in Christ."

4. **Live It Out**

- When faced with a trial this week, declare God's Word over the situation instead of agreeing with fear.
- Write down one area of your life where perseverance is being worked in you, and thank God daily for the victory that will come from it.
- Share with someone a testimony of how God has helped you endure and grow stronger through past challenges.

Reflection

_____

_____

_____

_____

_____

_____

_____

_____

_____

_____

_____

_____

_____

_____

_____

_____

_____

_____

_____

Week 23

Part 2: Character

Romans 5:3-4 *"And not only that, but we also glory in tribulations, knowing that tribulation produces perseverance; and perseverance,* **character***; and character, hope."*

In Greek, the word character means **"proof by trial; the state or disposition of that which has been tried and approved."** It refers to the refining process, much like the smelting away of dross from precious metals. When impurities are removed, only the pure metal remains. In the same way, when we endure suffering without wavering in our convictions, the dross-like aspects of our character are burned away, leaving only what is pure. As our character is refined, we begin to act, speak, and walk more like Jesus. This is the very purpose of the Refiner's fire: to burn away what is unnecessary so that what is essential may stand alone, clearly visible, front and center.

The Marine Corps has a saying: "Weakness is just pain leaving the body." It's used to motivate recruits during the grueling pain of boot camp, encouraging them not to give up. In my younger years, I didnt fully grasp the meaning of that phrase until recently. During the physical exertion required to become a Marine, recruits inevitably face pain. In those moments, they're given a choice: to yield to the pain and quit, or to push through it with a clear goal in mind. When they choose to press on, they increase their pain threshold—what once weakened them no longer has power. The weakness is gone, and strength remains.

So it is with our walk with the Lord. Enduring painful trials is the crucifixion of the flesh and the strengthening of the spirit. Pain, in this context, is just flesh leaving our soul.

Without undergoing this process of renewal, we will continue thinking the way the old man used to think, limited by what can be seen in the natural. That mindset is often shaped by our upbringing, molded by what was modeled for us, including destructive habits and patterns. But here's the incredible truth: we already have the mind of Christ!

1 Corinthians 2:16 *"For 'who has known the mind of the Lord that he may instruct Him?' But we have the mind of Christ."*

The mind of Christ resides within our born-again spirit and, according to **1 John 2:20**, it knows all things. Yet we cannot operate in the mind of Christ until we first reject the mind of the flesh. This is the very purpose of the furnace of affliction; its fire exposes deep-seated ways of thinking that may have remained hidden beneath the surface, unknown to our conscious awareness.

When those thoughts rise to the surface during trials, we must confront and reject them. We must silence their influence. We reject the patterns of our old thinking so that we can embrace God's thoughts, and align our minds with His Word. This requires speaking directly to those thoughts:

2 Corinthians 10:3–5 *"For though we walk in the flesh, we do not war according to the flesh. For the weapons of our warfare are not carnal but mighty in God for pulling down strongholds, casting down arguments and every high thing that exalts itself against the knowledge of God, bringing every thought into captivity to the obedience of Christ…"*

2 Corinthians 4:13 *"And since we have the same spirit of faith, according to what is written, 'I believed and therefore I spoke,' we also believe and therefore speak…"*

These strongholds are destructive mental patterns we've tolerated for too long. When they're exposed, we tear them down by declaring God's truth in their place. This is how we activate the mind of Christ within our spirit and release healing into our soul.

We already possess the power and authority, but that power must be released by speaking God's Word, regardless of how we feel. Carnal thinking leads to death, but the mind of Christ leads to life and peace:

Romans 8:6 *"For to be carnally minded is death, but to be spiritually minded is life and peace."*

When we begin to operate in the mind of Christ, we begin to reflect His character. Our actions, words, and decisions will mirror His. And when that happens, we'll walk in power, moving mountains everywhere we go.

Light for the Path

Character is forged in the fire of trials, burning away the old mindset of the flesh so that the mind of Christ within us shines through.

Deeper Light – Reflect + Respond

1. Read More

- Romans 5:3–4
- 1 Corinthians 2:16
- 2 Corinthians 10:3–5
- Romans 8:6
- 1 John 2:20

2. Journal Prompt

- What old thought patterns surface when I face trials?
- How can I actively replace those destructive mindsets with the truth of God's Word?
- In what ways have I already seen Christ's character formed in me through past refining seasons?

3. Daily Declaration of Faith

"I only have one way to go: UP! I know God is working all things together for my good, and I believe that the power to transform me is already within. I choose to believe it, speak it and walk in it regardless of how I feel."

4. **Live It Out**

- Identify one recurring negative thought pattern and speak a Scripture over it each time it arises.
- Write down three Scriptures that declare who you are in Christ and rehearse them daily this week.
- Share with someone how God is refining your thinking so you can encourage them in their own process.

Reflection

_____

_____

_____

_____

_____

_____

_____

_____

_____

_____

_____

_____

_____

_____

_____

_____

_____

_____

_____

_____

_____

Week 24

Part 3.1: Hope

> **Romans 5:3–4** *"And not only that, but we also glory in tribulations, knowing that tribulation produces perseverance; and perseverance, character; and character,* **hope.***"*

Now we arrive at the final point in this powerful progression: Hope. The entire purpose of enduring tribulations and walking through them victoriously is to bring us to this ultimate destination. Yet many people still don't understand the power of hope—so much so that Scripture places it alongside faith and love as one of the three greatest virtues of the Christian life (**1 Corinthians 13:13**).

In order to fully grasp what biblical hope truly is, we must first deconstruct the world's definition and rebuild our understanding based on the Word of God.

We have all heard it before, and maybe even said it ourselves:

"Well, I hope so."

However, if you pause and examine the condition of your heart when you say that phrase, you will often find that it was not said in faith. The world's version of hope is nothing more than wishful thinking, an emotional coping mechanism designed to protect the heart in case disappointment comes. That is why people say things like, **"Don't get your hopes up."** In other words, **"Don't believe too strongly because it might not happen, and you'll only end up hurt."**

These phrases were born out of pain, shaped by hearts that have endured deep disappointment affecting both speech and expectations. But this is not biblical hope.

Biblical hope is the confident expectation of good.

The operative word here is *expectation*. Every person lives with some form of expectation whether for good or bad. Biblical hope is grounded in the promises of God and believes they will come to pass. That's why the healing of our hearts is essential: when our hearts are healed, we are able to uproot negative expectations and replace them with the confident expectation of God's goodness.

It's a spiritual truth that we have passed from death to life (**John 5:24**). However, much of our thinking still needs to be renewed. We continue to think like the old, unredeemed man, and so we must intentionally renew our minds (**Romans 12:2**). If we don't, the enemy will use our past pain and disappointments to shape our expectations and that will ultimately influence our speech and behavior.

Proverbs 23:7a *"For as he thinks in his heart, so is he..."*

If we continually expect bad things to happen, those expectations will become the foundation of our thought life. And whatever fills the heart will eventually overflow from the mouth.

Luke 6:45 *"A good man out of the good treasure of his heart brings forth good; and an evil man out of the evil treasure of his heart brings forth evil. For out of the abundance of the heart his mouth speaks."*

So ask yourself: what is in abundance in your heart? If it's evil, pain, or disappointment, invite the Lord to heal it. Let Him replace it with good treasure. Then, no matter what you are facing, speak only what is good. Speak the Word!

Just as the body is nourished by what goes into the mouth, so your soul can be nourished by what comes out of your mouth. Use your words as a weapon. Speak against the residue of unbelief and fear until all that remains is the pure faith born out of your new nature in Christ.

Do not give up. Do not surrender to despair. You are being shaped and your character is being forged in the fire. The more you speak the

Word in the midst of pain, the more the mind of Christ is translating into your natural mind. But until you are convinced of God's love for you, until you believe you are truly worthy of that love, you will continue to expect what is bad instead of what is good. Your perception of unworthiness will block your ability to receive His blessings.

When you allow the love of God to transform your heart, from expecting evil to expecting only good, you will walk in true, unshakable hope. And Scripture promises:

Romans 5:5 *"…hope does not disappoint…"*

What does that really mean?

The Greek word for "**disappoint**" means **"to put to shame; to suffer repulse; to be let down by a hope that failed."** Let me illustrate with a simple example:

Imagine my son plays on his school's baseball team. Before a big game, I promise him, *"Son, I'll be there to watch you play."* Filled with confidence, he tells his friends and teachers, *"My dad's coming! He promised!"* However, if the game comes and goes and I never show up, his heart would sink. His friends might ask, *"I thought your dad was coming?"* and he would have no response. Not because he was wrong to believe, but because I failed to keep my word. That is what it means to be put to shame by hope that fails.

Now contrast that with God. When His love transforms us and we begin boldly speaking His promises, fully believing them with all our hearts, He always shows up. **ALWAYS!** He never breaks His word. His promises never fail. He will never cause you to hang your head in shame or regret.

Hebrews 2:15 *"And release those who through fear of death were all their lifetime subject to bondage."*

Before Christ, humanity lived in fear expecting only evil, judgment, and death. That fear enslaved them, shaping their minds like those of orphans and slaves. But Jesus came to destroy the devil and his works, and to deliver us from that bondage. He didn't just set us free, He made us royalty.

Slaves cannot inherit the promises of God because they cannot imagine themselves possessing them. They see themselves as unworthy, destined only for struggle and survival. But Scripture declares that we are no longer slaves, we are priests and kings unto our God, called to reign with Him on the earth.

Revelation 5:10 *"And have made us kings and priests to our God; and we shall reign on the earth."*

Romans 5:17 *"For if by the one man's offense death reigned through the one, much more those who receive abundance of grace and of the gift of righteousness will reign in life through the One, Jesus Christ."*

So rise up in faith. Receive the abundance of grace. Let God's love cast out every fear, and let biblical hope rise within you. Not wishful thinking, but confident expectation rooted in the unshakable promises of your faithful Father.

REMEMBER!

You were not made to barely get by.

You were made to REIGN.

LET HOPE ARISE

Light for the Path

Biblical hope is not wishful thinking; it is the confident expectation of God's goodness, rooted in His promises that never fail.

Deeper Light – Reflect + Respond

1. Read More

- Romans 5:3–5
- 1 Corinthians 13:13
- Romans 12:2
- Luke 6:45
- Revelation 5:10

2. Journal Prompt

- Do I see hope as "wishful thinking" or as confident expectation based on God's Word?
- What past disappointments still shape my expectations, and how can I invite the Lord to heal them?
- What promises of God do I need to begin declaring boldly over my life?

3. Daily Declaration of Faith

"I live in confident expectation of God's goodness. My hope in Christ will never be put to shame."

4. Live It Out

- Write down one promise of God you're believing for and speak it daily until it takes root in your heart.
- Replace every negative expectation this week with a declaration of God's goodness.
- Share with a friend or family member how God is shifting your heart from fear to hope.

Reflection

_____

_____

_____

_____

_____

_____

_____

_____

_____

_____

_____

_____

_____

_____

_____

_____

_____

_____

_____

Part 3.2: Hope

**"Revelation is the unveiling of what God has prepared. When the
heart sees it, hope becomes unshakable."**

Andrew Murray

Another way to define biblical hope is that it is entirely dependent
upon your ability to see with the eyes of your heart. In other
words, hope is the result of divine revelation. The issue many face is
that they have closed the eyes of their heart due to the pain and trauma
encountered in life. This leads to a hardening of the heart, which dulls
spiritual sensitivity and makes it difficult to discern truth clearly
(**Matthew 13:15**). As a result, people often expect bad things to
happen, because their perception is filtered through the lens of their
past wounds.

However, when we allow God to cleanse and heal our hearts, our
capacity to receive revelation of His Word begins to expand. Consider
the prayer of Paul in Ephesians:

Ephesians 1:17–18 *"That the God of our Lord Jesus Christ, the Father of
glory, may give to you the spirit of wisdom and revelation in the knowledge of Him,
the eyes of your understanding being enlightened; that you may know what is
the hope of His calling..."*

The phrase *"the eyes of your understanding being enlightened"* speaks of
spiritual sight—Revelation. Notice the order: hope comes after
revelation. If you have ever experienced a moment when a familiar
scripture suddenly came alive where you saw it inwardly and it made
perfect sense, that was revelation. The fruit of that moment is

a confident expectation that what God says is yours. You can now say with conviction, *"I see what the Word says, and I know it's mine. I already have it!"*

This is what it means to see with the eyes of your heart: to perceive and grasp spiritual truth inwardly. Receiving anything from God, even salvation, hinges on this ability to see. Once we truly see what the Word says, and fresh hope begins to rise in our hearts, we are empowered to speak it forth in faith and expect it to manifest, just as Jesus taught in **Mark 11:22–24.**

This is why Scripture exhorts us:

Hebrews 10:23 *"Let us hold fast the confession of our hope without wavering, for He who promised is faithful."*

Hope will never put us to shame, because God is always faithful to His Word.

Jesus expressed this same truth:

John 15:7 *"If you abide in Me, and My words abide in you, you will ask what you desire, and it shall be done for you."*

Here, the Greek word for **"words"** is **"Rhema"**, which means the spoken word. Rhema denotes the moment when the Spirit of God speaks a specific word into your situation. It can also refer to a moment when you are reading Scripture and the Holy Spirit quickens a verse to your heart, He lifts it off the page and speaks it directly to you. This is revelation when God speaks, and your spiritual ears hear it. Revelation is always the fruit of Rhema to those who have ears to hear.

When we receive that Rhema word and the hope it produces, we can boldly speak it out, fully expecting it to come to pass. But again, it all begins with the ability to see.

Those who reject the gospel, and scriptural truths, are often described in Scripture as spiritually blind:

2 Corinthians 4:3–4 *"But even if our gospel is veiled, it is veiled to those who are perishing, whose minds the god of this age has blinded, who do not believe, lest the light of the gospel of the glory of Christ, who is the image of God, should shine on them."*

Spiritual blindness is the inability to perceive God's truth because of hardness of heart, unbelief, sin, or deception. Though they may have physical sight, they have closed themselves off to spiritual realities.

Matthew 13:15 *"For the hearts of this people have grown dull. Their ears are hard of hearing, And their eyes they have closed, Lest they should see with their eyes and hear with their ears, Lest they should understand with their hearts and turn, So that I should heal them."*

This is why we must continually pray as the psalmist did:

Psalm 119:18 *"Open my eyes, that I may see wondrous things from Your law."*

Hope is a direct result of receiving revelation from God's Word. And as children of God, we've already been given access:

Matthew 13:11 *"He answered and said to them, 'Because it has been given to you to know the mysteries of the kingdom of heaven, but to them it has not been given.'"*

Therefore, we must continually pursue deeper levels of revelation in the Word never growing discouraged, but allowing the Lord to refine our hearts. In this process, He forms in us the strength and character required to walk faithfully with Him all our days.

Psalm 36:9 *"For with You is the fountain of life; In Your light we see light."*

Light for the Path

Hope is born from revelation, when the eyes of our heart are opened to see God's truth, we gain unshakable confidence in His promises.

Deeper Light – Reflect + Respond

1. Read More

- Ephesians 1:17–18
- Hebrews 10:23
- John 15:7
- 2 Corinthians 4:3–6
- Psalm 119:18

2. Journal Prompt

- What areas of my heart feel hardened by pain or disappointment, making it difficult to "see" with spiritual eyes?
- When was the last time God's Word became revelation to me, and how did it reshape my hope?
- Have I been asking God to open the eyes of my understanding daily, believing He desires to do so?

3. Daily Declaration of Faith

"The eyes of my heart are open to see the hope of His calling. God's Word is alive in me."

4. **Live It Out**

- Begin each day this week by praying Psalm 119:18: 'Open my eyes, that I may see wondrous things from Your law.'
- Write down one Scripture that God highlights to you and declare it out loud as a Rhema word over your life.
- Share with a trusted believer how God has opened your eyes in a specific area, and encourage them to ask for fresh revelation too.

Reflection

_____

_____

_____

_____

_____

_____

_____

_____

_____

_____

_____

_____

_____

_____

_____

_____

_____

_____

IDENTITY *and* AUTHORITY *in* CHRIST

Weeks 26-31

Week 26

Ambassadors of Heaven

> **2 Corinthians 5:20** *"Now then, we are ambassadors for Christ, as though God were pleading through us: we implore you on Christ's behalf, be reconciled to God."*

In this verse, Paul describes himself as an ambassador for Christ. But what exactly does that mean, and how does it apply to the role we play in the Kingdom of Heaven?

Let's explore the key responsibilities of a natural ambassador:

I.   **Official Representative** – An ambassador acts as the official representative of the government they serve.

II. **Diplomatic Liaison** – They serve as the primary communication link between their home nation and the foreign land they reside in.

III. **Defender of Citizens** – They safeguard the interests and well-being of citizens from their home country who are living or traveling in the host nation.

IV. **Negotiator** – They engage in diplomatic negotiations on behalf of their home government.

In other words, an ambassador is someone sent to live in a foreign land while carrying the authority and voice of the government they represent. When they speak, it's as though their leader is speaking through them. This is who Paul says we are!

We have been sent by the Kingdom of Heaven to live here temporarily, representing Heaven's interests and inviting others to become citizens of that Kingdom. This is why it's crucial that we do not become entangled in or enamored by the affairs and attractions of this world.

To do so would be to assimilate into the culture of the host nation making us ineffective in our true purpose.

2 Timothy 2:4 *"No one engaged in warfare entangles himself with the affairs of this life, that he may please him who enlisted him as a soldier."*

1 John 2:15-16 *"Do not love the world or the things in the world. If anyone loves the world, the love of the Father is not in him."*

Matthew 13:22 *"Now he who received seed among the thorns is he who hears the word, and the cares of this world and the deceitfulness of riches choke the word, and he becomes unfruitful."*

Ambassadors also carry a special legal protection called diplomatic immunity. Here's what it includes:

I.   Ambassadors cannot be arrested or detained, even if accused of a crime.
II.   They are exempt from the host nation's court system.
III. Police cannot enter their residence without permission.
IV.   They enjoy tax-exempt status.

As ambassadors of Heaven, we too have a type of heavenly diplomatic immunity. That doesn't mean trials won't come because the enemy does not obey God's laws. He will try to trespass unless we enforce the authority and freedom we've been given. But the Word assures us:

Isaiah 54:15 *"Indeed they shall surely assemble, but not because of Me. Whoever assembles against you shall fall for your sake."*

This means the attack may come, but it is not sent by God. In fact, just before that verse, God says:

Isaiah 54:9-10 *"For this is like the waters of Noah to Me; For as I have sworn That the waters of Noah would no longer cover the earth, So have I sworn That I would not be angry with you, nor rebuke you…But My kindness shall not depart from you, Nor shall My covenant of peace be removed," Says the Lord, who has mercy on you."*

We have a covenant with God that is everlasting! Sadly, many Christians have more faith in the promise that God will never flood the earth again than in the truth that our sins have been fully atoned for. But Scripture affirms that our new covenant through the blood of Jesus (**Luke 22:20**) is just as sure as His promise to Noah.

That covenant declares: God will not be angry with us, nor will He rebuke us. We are His beloved children, and our sins, once a barrier between Him and us, have been removed through Christ.

So don't let anyone tell you that sickness, lack, or pain is God's way of teaching or punishing you. His Word is clear:

James 1:13, 16-17 *"Let no one say when he is tempted, 'I am tempted by God'; for God cannot be tempted by evil, nor does He Himself tempt anyone... Do not be deceived, my beloved brethren. Every good gift and every perfect gift is from above, and comes down from the Father of lights, with whom there is no variation or shadow of turning."*

God does not use evil to teach us, He teaches us through His Word. If we walk a painful path, He may use it to instruct us, but He is never the author of that pain.

Therefore, we are ambassadors sent from Heaven on a mission to bring the lost into the Kingdom of our King. And unlike earthly ambassadors who enjoy temporary benefits, our spiritual privileges are eternal and far more powerful.

Let's walk in the confidence of our identity and inheritance!

Light for the Path

As ambassadors of Heaven, we carry the authority and message of our King, living in the world but representing the interests and covenant of God's Kingdom.

Deeper Light – Reflect + Respond

1. Read More

- Luke 10:19
- Isaiah 51:16
- Psalm 18:2
- Isaiah 54:9–15
- 1 John 5:18

2. Journal Prompt

- How do I see myself: as just a citizen of earth, or as an ambassador of Heaven?
- What "cares of this world" have tried to entangle me and make me ineffective?
- Where do I need to begin walking in my covenant confidence and heavenly authority?

3. Daily Declaration of Faith

"I am an ambassador of Christ. I carry the authority of Heaven and represent my Father's Kingdom on earth."

4. **Live It Out**

- Identify one worldly entanglement or distraction and surrender it to God this week.
- Speak boldly to yourself daily: "I am an ambassador of Heaven, carrying Christ's authority."
- Share the message of reconciliation with someone in your life who needs to hear the hope of Christ.

Reflection

_____

_____

_____

_____

_____

_____

_____

_____

_____

_____

_____

_____

_____

_____

_____

_____

_____

_____

Heaven Backs You Up: You Have the Authority

Matthew 18:18 *"Assuredly, I say to you, whatever you bind on earth will be bound in heaven, and whatever you loose on earth will be loosed in heaven."*

Notice how this scripture presents two perspectives: man's perspective on earth and God's perspective in heaven. Whatever man decides on earth, God confirms in heaven. This verse reveals that God has delegated real authority to mankind to choose for himself. God will never override man's ability to choose. As free moral agents, we are accountable for our choices, and God simply confirms them.

However, many people become confused when interpreting certain scriptures and, as a result, develop doctrines that misrepresent God's nature. This misunderstanding often comes from failing to distinguish between these two perspectives. Let's take a look at an example:

Romans 13:1 *"Let every soul be subject to the governing authorities. For there is no authority except from God, and the authorities that exist are appointed by God."*

Some people mistakenly believe this verse teaches that God controls everything including political leadership and therefore conclude that their vote doesn't matter. They'll say, *"See? God appoints our leaders, so why bother voting?"* Those thoughts stem from a misunderstanding of the passage. Remember, many see God's works, but few understand His ways (**Hebrews 3:10**).

So let me ask the question: Does God personally elect our leaders? Does He override human decisions and install rulers without our input? No. We choose our leaders and God appoints them because we have chosen them. Here's a biblical example to consider:

1 Samuel 8:6–9 *"But the thing displeased Samuel when they said, 'Give us a king to judge us.' So Samuel prayed to the Lord. And the Lord said to Samuel, 'Heed the voice of the people in all that they say to you; for they have not rejected you, but they have rejected Me, that I should not reign over them… Now therefore, heed their voice. However, you shall solemnly forewarn them, and show them the behavior of the king who will reign over them.'"*

God intended to reign over Israel Himself, but the people demanded a human king. Did God say, **"Absolutely not! I'm your King and this is not happening!"** No. If He had, He would have become like a dictator who refuses to allow free will. Instead, God honored their request. He gave them Saul as king but only after they had already chosen him in their hearts.

This brings us back to our opening verse, emphasizing the authority we hold:

Matthew 18:18 *"Assuredly, I say to you, whatever you bind on earth will be bound in heaven, and whatever you loose on earth will be loosed in heaven."*

Heaven backs what we bind and loose as if God had made the decision Himself. This is the weight of the authority He's entrusted to mankind. And with that authority comes great responsibility.

Some will quote another verse in Romans to suggest that God is ultimately in control of who is saved or condemned:

Romans 9:18 *"Therefore He has mercy on whom He wills, and whom He wills He hardens."*

Paul uses Pharaoh as an example of someone whose heart was hardened by God. It is important to understand that Pharaoh first hardened his own heart. When someone rejects the manifest presence of God, they become hardened in proportion to the revelation they reject. Imagine a scale—when God reveals Himself in a greater measure and someone still refuses Him, the scales tip equally toward hardening.

In Pharaoh's case, God revealed Himself through undeniable signs and wonders, yet Pharaoh resisted. His heart grew so hard that he thought he could overpower the Israelites even to the point of chasing them into the parted Red Sea. That kind of delusion ultimately led to his downfall, as the waters collapsed over him and his army.

Hardening, then, is not arbitrary, it is a consequence. God simply confirms people in the path they have already chosen.

Romans 13:2 AMPC *"Therefore he who resists and sets himself up against the authorities resists what God has appointed and arranged [in divine order]. And those who resist will bring down judgment upon themselves [receiving the penalty due them]."*

This reinforces the truth: God is the power source but we decide when to flip the switch.

Consider this additional verse:

2 Peter 3:9 *"The Lord is not slack concerning His promise, as some count slackness, but is longsuffering toward us, not willing that any should perish but that all should come to repentance."*

God desires that all be saved but not all will be. Why? Because His desire does not override our ability to choose. People go to hell by their own decision. God does not force anyone into heaven. He isn't like a mother pushing her reluctant child through the doorway of a dental office. He honors people's decision to choose destruction if that is what they want.

You might ask, *"Well, if someone chooses God when they stand before Him, won't He accept them then?"* No, because only faith pleases God. And when you're standing in front of Him, faith is no longer required. As long as we are alive in this body, we have the opportunity to believe by faith. After that, the opportunity is gone.

Here's another commonly misunderstood verse:

Romans 9:20–21 *"But indeed, O man, who are you to reply against God? Will the thing formed say to him who formed it, 'Why have you made me like this?' Does not the potter have power over the clay, from the same lump to make one vessel for honor and another for dishonor?"*

At first glance, this seems to suggest that God preordains some for destruction and others for salvation. But let's look at another passage that brings clarity:

2 Timothy 2:20–21 *"But in a great house there are not only vessels of gold and silver, but also of wood and clay, some for honor and some for dishonor. Therefore if anyone cleanses himself from the latter, he will be a vessel for honor, sanctified and useful for the Master, prepared for every good work."*

Here, Paul makes it clear: **"If anyone cleanses himself…"**—it's a choice. We determine the kind of vessel we become. Yes, we may have inherited pain, brokenness, or sin from life's circumstances but we still have the power to choose obedience, repentance, and transformation. Scripture does not teach that God assigns us a fixed fate without our consent.

To confirm this, ask yourself: Is there any example in Scripture where someone sincerely chose to obey God, but God forced them into disobedience by hardening their heart? No! Such an example does not exist. We have the authority to choose the course of our lives. And whatever choice we make, whether for life or death, heaven will honor it.

Deuteronomy 30:19 *"I call heaven and earth as witnesses today against you, that I have set before you life and death, blessing and cursing; therefore choose life, that both you and your descendants may live;"*

Light for the Path

God has given us real authority to choose, and heaven confirms our decisions—life or death, blessing or cursing—the responsibility rests with us.

Deeper Light – Reflect + Respond

1. Read More

- Matthew 18:18
- Romans 13:1–2
- 1 Samuel 8:6–9
- 2 Peter 3:9
- Deuteronomy 30:19

2. Journal Prompt

- Do I live as though my choices carry eternal weight, or do I assume God will override them?
- Where have I allowed confusion or misunderstanding of Scripture to excuse passivity in my decisions?
- What area of my life is God calling me to "choose life" today?

3. Daily Declaration of Faith

"I choose life. Heaven confirms my decisions, and I walk in the authority God has entrusted to me."

4. **Live It Out**

- This week, intentionally "choose life" in one area, whether through forgiveness, obedience, or faith, and declare that choice in prayer.
- When you face a decision, pause and ask: Does this bind me to the flesh or loose me into God's Spirit?
- Encourage someone struggling with doubt by reminding them that God always honors the decision to choose Him.

Reflection

The Power of Sonship

John 5:19–23 *"Then Jesus answered and said to them, 'Most assuredly, I say to you, the Son can do nothing of Himself, but what He sees the Father do; for whatever He does, the Son also does in like manner. For the Father loves the Son, and shows Him all things that He Himself does; and He will show Him greater works than these, that you may marvel. For as the Father raises the dead and gives life to them, even so the Son gives life to whom He will. For the Father judges no one, but has committed all judgment to the Son, that all should honor the Son just as they honor the Father. He who does not honor the Son does not honor the Father who sent Him.'"*

In this passage, Jesus is speaking in a way that would have been deeply significant to His Jewish audience. But to us in the West, the full impact can be easily missed because we don't share the same cultural framework. What Jesus is doing here is describing a well-known and honored concept in Jewish tradition: the transition of a father's estate to his son.

In Jewish culture, sons were considered equal to their fathers in status and authority for several reasons. Typically, a son would inherit the father's estate and authority upon the father's death. However, the father could also voluntarily delegate aspects of his estate, legal authority, judgment, and representation while still alive. This is exactly what Jesus is describing in these verses:

John 5:22 *"For the Father judges no one, but has committed all judgment to the Son."*

Jesus is explaining a divine delegation of authority. The Father has entrusted Him with judgment, a sacred responsibility. This level of intimacy with the Father was unprecedented and caused great offense to the religious leaders of His day. Just a few chapters later, they attempt to stone Him for making Himself equal with God. But the roots of that declaration are planted in these very verses.

In Jewish thought, a son wasn't just biologically connected to the father; he shared his nature and essence. He didn't merely follow in his father's footsteps, he stood in his place, carried his name, and upheld his honor. The son became the father's legal and relational representative. To honor the son was to honor the father. To disregard the son was to insult the father.

This is what Jesus is unveiling. As the Son, He carries the Father's authority, speaks on His behalf, and conducts His legal affairs on earth. This wasn't a poetic metaphor—this was a bold claim to divine identity and authority. As with Abraham, Isaac, and Jacob, the covenantal inheritance passes from the father down to the son, affirming continuity and equality in status before God.

In ancient Jewish law, a faithful son could represent his father's will with full legal force. When he spoke, it was as if the father himself were speaking. Jesus applies this cultural reality to Himself:

John 10:28–30 *"And I give them eternal life, and they shall never perish; neither shall anyone snatch them out of My hand. My Father, who has given them to Me, is greater than all; and no one is able to snatch them out of My Father's hand. I and My Father are one."*

To Jesus' Jewish listeners, this was a staggering claim. By referring to God as His Father, He was declaring that He was equal in nature, authority, and inheritance. As the Firstborn, He was claiming the right to the Father's entire estate, sent to carry out divine business on earth. His words carried the same weight, power, and binding authority as the Father Himself.

John 14:9 *"Jesus said to him, 'Have I been with you so long, and yet you have not known Me, Philip? He who has seen Me has seen the Father; so how can you say, 'Show us the Father'?'"*

Jesus is the Son of God sent from the courts of Heaven to conduct legal matters on earth, to reverse the guilty verdict of sin, and to make a way for all of us to be restored to sonship through Him, our elder Brother. As the Firstborn, He receives the double portion of honor and inheritance:

Romans 8:29 *"For whom He foreknew, He also predestined to be conformed to the image of His Son, that He might be the firstborn among many brethren."*

Because Jesus was sent by the Father, He carried the full authority of the Father's estate. And now, the amazing part is this:

John 20:21 *"So Jesus said to them again, 'Peace to you! As the Father has sent Me, I also send you.'"*

Through Christ, we are now one with the Father (**John 17:21**), and we have been sent, commissioned to represent Heaven, just as Jesus did. As sons and daughters adopted into His family, we too carry the authority of the Father's estate in Christ.

John 17:18 *"As You sent Me into the world, I also have sent them into the world."*

This means we now represent the Father's estate and Kingdom, carrying the full weight of His authority behind what we say and do. The same authority that Jesus walked in during His time on earth has now been given to us. That's why He clearly stated:

John 14:12 *"Most assuredly, I say to you, he who believes in Me, the works that I do he will do also; and greater works than these he will do, because I go to My Father."*

We have been made sons of God, just as Jesus was declared to be, and we now share in that same authority. We must take hold of this truth, that we may go forth and carry out the work of the Kingdom while it is still day.

Light for the Path

Through Christ, we are restored to sonship, sharing in the Father's authority, carrying His name, and representing His Kingdom on earth.

Deeper Light – Reflect + Respond

1. Read More

- John 5:19-24
- John 6:38-40
- John 7:16-18
- John 17:1-26
- Matthew 28:18-20

2. Journal Prompt

- Do I see myself merely as a servant of God, or as a son/daughter with full inheritance rights in Christ?
- What would change in my daily life if I fully believed I carried the authority of the Father's estate?
- How can I begin to walk more boldly in the authority and identity Jesus has given me?

3. Daily Declaration of Faith

"I am a child of God, sent in the authority of my Father's Kingdom. Greater works I will do through Christ."

4. **Live It Out**

- Speak a declaration each day this week: "I am a son/daughter of God, sent to represent His Kingdom."
- Step into one situation with boldness where you've previously held back, exercising your authority in Christ.
- Share with someone how understanding your sonship is changing the way you live.

Reflection

_____

_____

_____

_____

_____

_____

_____

_____

_____

_____

_____

_____

_____

_____

_____

_____

_____

_____

_____

_____

THE POWER OF ATTENTIVE EARS

Mark 4:23–25 (NLT) *"Anyone with ears to hear should listen and understand. Then he added, 'Pay close attention to what you hear. The closer you listen, the more understanding you will be given, and you will receive even more. To those who listen to my teaching, more understanding will be given. But for those who are not listening, even what little understanding they have will be taken away from them.'"*

Listening brings a reward. According to this passage, Jesus told His disciples that listening is the key to receiving. He urged them to listen, to pay close attention, and to lean in even closer to His teaching.

There is also a clear warning from Jesus for those who do not listen closely to His words. The understanding they already have will be taken away from them. That is a sobering thought. In the world we live in, it often seems as though understanding and knowledge that once guided people has faded away. Could it be that many have refused to listen to the teachings of the Messiah and are now experiencing exactly what He warned about?

The instructions and warnings found in Scripture are always for our benefit. Behind every command Jesus gives, whether to do something or to refrain from it, there is always a promise. Here, He wanted us to understand that listening is the key to increase in every way. In contrast, refusing to listen leads to loss. Those who close their ears to His words eventually lose even what they already have.

The Bible contains many verses urging us to listen carefully to what Jesus is saying.

Matthew 11:15 (NLT) *"Anyone with ears to hear should listen and understand!"*

Luke 8:8 (NLT) *"Still other seed fell on fertile soil. This seed grew and produced a crop that was a hundred times as much as had been planted!" When he had said this, he called out, "Anyone with ears to hear should listen and understand."*

This repeated instruction to listen shows how important it was for Jesus to emphasize this point. He knew that truly listening to His words would lead to a reward—an eternal reward of spiritual maturity, understanding, and knowledge. He also knew that for those who chose to close their ears to His teaching, there would be consequences.

His continual urging, **"Anyone with ears to hear should listen and understand,"** was a heartfelt plea for people to receive all that He came to offer and not risk losing the blessings they had already gained.

Keep your ears tuned to the voice of Jesus, for in His words are treasures beyond imagination; more than your heart could ever dream of receiving.

Light for the Path

Attentive listening to Jesus opens the door to deeper understanding and increase, but ignoring His words leads to loss.

Deeper Light – Reflect + Respond

1. Read More

- Mark 4:21–25
- Matthew 13:11-16
- Luke 8:18
- Proverbs 4:20–22
- Hebrews 2:1

2. Journal Prompt

- How closely am I listening to what Jesus is speaking to me through His Word and Spirit?
- Have there been areas in my life where I've neglected His voice and lost clarity as a result?
- What practical steps can I take to tune my ears more consistently to His voice?

3. Daily Declaration of Faith

"I have ears to hear and a heart to understand. As I listen to Jesus, He gives me greater revelation."

4. Live It Out

- Set aside 10–15 minutes daily this week to read a passage of Scripture slowly, asking the Holy Spirit to highlight one word or phrase.
- Write down what you sense God speaking and revisit it throughout the day as a reminder.
- Declare over your life; "Above all else, I will guard my heart because when I do, I guard my ability to hear the Lord's voice."

Reflection

_____

_____

_____

_____

_____

_____

_____

_____

_____

_____

_____

_____

_____

_____

_____

_____

_____

_____

_____

Week 30

The Power of Gratitude

1 Corinthians 15:57 *"But thanks be to God, who gives us the victory through our Lord Jesus Christ."*

Gratitude is more than a polite response, it is a supernatural key. It is what pulls on the promise and brings the fulfillment into manifestation. When we give thanks, we are saying by faith, *"I believe I've already received it."* Gratitude is an expression of trust, a declaration that God is faithful to His Word.

Mark 11:24 *"Therefore I say to you, whatever things you ask when you pray, believe that you receive them, and you will have them."*

Gratitude is an act of faith, being thankful before the manifestation appears. It positions our hearts to receive. Often, we learn true gratitude in seasons of lack. In those moments, God provides for us frequently through others and we're given a choice: to respond with humility or pride. Gratitude humbly receives the blessing, no matter how it comes. Pride, on the other hand, rejects help because it couldn't produce the provision on its own.

Learning gratitude in seasons of lack is the training ground for increase. It's how we rise in every area, especially financially. The more grateful we are when we have little, the more grounded we'll be when we have much. Gratitude ensures that wealth never owns us. It cultivates a character that remains unshaken by increase. We become the kind of people who walk in abundance yet carry humility, so much so, that others might never guess we have millions in the bank. Why? Because we haven't changed, our hearts remain rooted in thankfulness.

Philippians 4:6–7 *"Be anxious for nothing, but in everything by prayer and supplication, with thanksgiving, let your requests be made known to God; and the peace of God, which surpasses all understanding, will guard your hearts and minds through Christ Jesus."*

Notice the link between thanksgiving and peace. The Greek word for peace here is **"eirēnē"**, the equivalent of the Hebrew word shalom, which means: **"nothing missing, nothing broken."** When we thank God, this peace, shalom, guards our hearts and minds. It's not merely a sense of calm while we wait. It is a supernatural condition of wholeness.

Isaiah 53:5 *"But He was wounded for our transgressions, He was bruised for our iniquities; the chastisement for our peace was upon Him…"*

Jesus was chastised so we could be made whole. God always intended to restore us to a state where nothing is missing and nothing is broken, but He needed a perfect man to be chastised in the place of imperfect men. That man was Jesus. Because of Him, we now live under a covenant where healing, freedom, provision, and wholeness are our reality.

Do you need healing? Provision? Restoration in your family or heart? These things are not far from you. They're already provided in Christ and gratitude is the pull on the promise. As we walk in thankfulness, we attract the fulfillment of every need, because we're living from a posture of faith.

2 Peter 1:2–4 *"Grace and peace be multiplied to you in the knowledge of God and of Jesus our Lord, as His divine power has given to us all things that pertain to life and godliness, through the knowledge of Him who called us by glory and virtue, by which have been given to us exceedingly great and precious promises, that through these you may be partakers of the divine nature…"*

You already have every promise in Christ. Gratitude is what draws it from the unseen into the seen. It's not momentary, it's a lifestyle. It transforms lack into preparation, and abundance into ministry. It anchors us through every season, proving that thankfulness isn't just good manners it's kingdom strategy.

Light for the Path

Gratitude is a supernatural act of faith; it pulls unseen promises into reality and anchors our hearts in God's peace and provision.

Deeper Light – Reflect + Respond

1. Read More

- 1 Corinthians 15:57
- Mark 11:24
- Philippians 4:6–7
- Isaiah 53:5
- 2 Peter 1:2–4

2. Journal Prompt

- How do I usually respond in seasons of lack; with gratitude and humility, or with frustration and pride?
- What promise of God am I believing for right now, and how can I begin thanking Him in advance for it?
- How has gratitude already shifted my perspective in past seasons of need or abundance?

3. Daily Declaration of Faith

"I give thanks in all things. Gratitude draws God's promises into my life and fills me with His peace."

4. **Live It Out**

- Each day this week, write down three specific things you are thankful for, especially in areas where you are still waiting on breakthrough.
- When tempted to complain, pause and turn your words into thanks.
- Share with a friend or family member one way you've seen gratitude unlock peace or provision in your life.

Reflection

_____

_____

_____

_____

_____

_____

_____

_____

_____

_____

_____

_____

_____

_____

_____

_____

_____

_____

The Power of Love

"The only power that can overcome the flesh is the fire of divine love."

Leonard Ravenhill

Love is the force that keeps the human heart from being overcome by the damaging effects of pain. When we walk in love, we are operating in a higher dimension, one that pain cannot touch. Yes, we will still feel the sting of hardship, just as God Himself grieves over the death of the wicked (**Ezekiel 33:11**). But that pain will not be permitted to mold us into a diminished version of who we were created to be, as it does for so many in the world. Instead of being dominated by what dominates others, we are empowered to rise above it.

Romans 8:35, 37 *"Who shall separate us from the love of Christ? Shall tribulation, or distress, or persecution, or famine, or nakedness, or peril, or sword? … Yet in all these things we are more than conquerors through Him who loved us."*

Nothing in life has the authority to sever us from the love of our Father. No tribulation, pressure, or difficulty can break our intimacy with Him. Distress, persecution, financial strain, shame, poverty, threats, even physical affliction, hold no ultimate power over us. Why? Because our connection to God, rooted in His love, enables us to live above the challenges of life. It gives us the perspective we need to see rightly.

Most of life's difficulties feel unbearable because we are focused on the problem instead of the Lord. When we fix our eyes on the problem, it grows in our mind and begins to dominate us. But when we set our gaze on the Lord, even if we are walking through hell, we walk in victory. God's love bestows worth upon us, and from that worth comes the boldness and courage to face anything with Him.

2 Corinthians 4:8–9 *"We are hard-pressed on every side, yet not crushed; we are perplexed, but not in despair; persecuted, but not forsaken; struck down, but not destroyed."*

Paul endured intense persecution, but he never allowed the pressure to define him. He held a heavenly perspective. That's the kind of man who cannot be stopped. Having the right perspective in hardship and remaining grounded in God's unfailing love is the secret to walking in victory in every circumstance. But love is not alone in this battle.

Love has a companion: forgiveness.

To love is to forgive, and to forgive is to love. The two cannot be separated. Forgiveness is the shield we place over our hearts to guard them from the enemy's attempts to wound us through pain. When we forgive, we mirror God. We walk in freedom, unbound by the enemy's cords of bitterness, rage, and offense.

Forgiveness is extending the same mercy and love we have received. We reflect the glory of God most clearly when we forgive freely, just as Christ did, crying out from the cross:

Luke 23:24 *"Father, forgive them, for they know not what they do."*

When we forgive, we become untouchable and unassailable by the enemy. He cannot fasten hooks in our soul to manipulate and control us. We are free—free from bitterness, rage, malice, revenge, and all destructive forces. We step into our divine calling as image bearers of the Most High, who is both a loving Father and a Victorious Warrior.

We were made for this. Born for this. Destined for this.

Arise and shine in that calling! The world is counting on you!

Isaiah 60:1–2 *"Arise, shine; For your light has come! And the glory of the Lord is risen upon you. For behold, the darkness shall cover the earth, And deep darkness the people; But the Lord will arise over you, And His glory will be seen upon you."*

Confession of faith

"The love of God enables me to dominate what once dominated me; it empowers me to walk upon the very waves that once threatened to drown me as I turn my eyes away from the storm and fix them on His loving gaze."

Light for the Path

God's love empowers us to rise above pain and hardship, and forgiveness keeps our hearts free from the enemy's grip.

Deeper Light – Reflect + Respond

1. Read More

- Romans 8:35–39
- Mark 11:25
- Luke 23:34
- Colossians 3:12–14
- Isaiah 60:1–2

2. Journal Prompt

- Where am I allowing pain, offense, or bitterness to shape me instead of God's love?
- How has unforgiveness limited my freedom, and what would it look like to release it?
- What does it mean for me personally to "arise and shine" in God's love right now?

3. Daily Declaration of Faith

> *"Nothing can separate me from the love of Christ. I forgive freely and walk in God's victory."*

4. Live It Out

- Ask God to reveal one person you need to forgive, then release them in prayer this week.
- Speak out loud a declaration daily: "Nothing can separate me from the love of Christ."
- Look for one opportunity to actively love someone who is difficult or hurting, showing them God's heart through your actions.

Reflection

_____

_____

_____

_____

_____

_____

_____

_____

_____

_____

_____

_____

_____

_____

_____

_____

_____

_____

_____

_____

GUARDING AGAINST SPIRITUAL PITFALLS

Weeks 32–39

PRIDE

Mark 14:27–29 (ERV) *Then Jesus told the followers, "You will all lose your faith. The Scriptures say, 'I will kill the shepherd, and the sheep will run away.' But after I am killed, I will rise from death. Then I will go to Galilee. I will be there before you go there." Peter said, "All the other followers may lose their faith, but I will not."*

Pride is what wars against truth.

But the **fear of the Lord** removes pride and **honors the truth**.

This moment between Jesus and Peter is a clear confirmation that truth will always prevail over pride. Jesus plainly foretold that all the disciples would stumble, yet Peter and the others refused to believe it. Still, the outcome was exactly as foretold: Peter denied Jesus three times, and the disciples scattered, fulfilling the prophecy spoken in Zechariah:

Zechariah 13:7 (NLT) *"Awake, O sword, against my shepherd, the man who is my partner," says the Lord of Heaven's Armies. "Strike down the shepherd, and the sheep will be scattered, and I will turn against the lambs."*

What was it in Peter that made him think he knew better than his Messiah? The answer is in his response:

"All the other followers may lose their faith, but my faith will never be shaken."

This is the language of pride.

Proverbs 16:18 *"Pride goes before destruction, and a haughty spirit before a fall."*

Pride says, *"You do not know my future, Jesus. That is not my character. I will never do what You say I will do."*

But **humility** and **holy fear** say the opposite:

"I may not like what You are saying, Jesus, but I know You cannot lie. So I choose to believe You, even when Your words seem painful or hard to accept."

Hebrews 6:18 (NLT) *"So God has given both his promise and his oath. These two things are unchangeable because it is impossible for God to lie. Therefore, we who have fled to Him for refuge can have great confidence as we hold to the hope that lies before us."*

If we live in pride, we will continually resist the very truths Jesus speaks. This reveals a lack of the reverent fear of the Lord that draws us deeper into fellowship with Him. Like Peter, when we resist truth, it does not change the outcome. Truth will still stand, and pride will still fall.

So why not yield to the One who is Truth Himself? Why not believe every word He speaks, knowing that He is always faithful?

1 Corinthians 1:9 *"God is faithful, by whom you were called into the fellowship of His Son, Jesus Christ our Lord."*

When we choose to walk in **holy fear**, pride is stripped away and **truth is honored** in our lives.

Light for the Path

Pride resists truth and leads to a fall, but holy fear humbly receives God's Word, knowing He cannot lie.

Deeper Light – Reflect + Respond

1. Read More

- Mark 14:27–31
- Zechariah 13:7
- Proverbs 16:18
- Hebrews 6:18
- 1 Corinthians 1:9

2. Journal Prompt

- In what ways do I sometimes think I know better than Jesus?
- Where has pride caused me to resist a truth I didn't want to hear?
- How can walking in holy fear reshape the way I respond to God's Word?

3. Daily Declaration of Faith

"I humble myself before the Lord. I believe His Word, for He cannot lie, and His truth stands in my life."

4. Live It Out

- As an act of faith, declare this word over your life; *"The wisdom of the Lord is mine, when I have a holy fear of the Lord!"*
- Confess one area where pride has shaped your words or actions, and invite God to correct it.
- Practice listening more than speaking in a conversation, as an act of humility.

Reflection

_____

_____

_____

_____

_____

_____

_____

_____

_____

_____

_____

_____

_____

_____

_____

_____

_____

_____

_____

STUBBORN UNBELIEF

Mark 16:13 (NLT) *"They returned and told the rest, but they did not believe them either."*

What could cause the close, trusted followers of Jesus to disbelieve the testimony of His resurrection?

According to **Mark 16:10**, their grief and weeping clouded their faith. Instead of remembering the promises Jesus had spoken to them, not once, but at least three times (see **Mark 8:31, 9:31, 10:33–34**), they were consumed with sorrow, devastated by what appeared to be the end of everything they had hoped for.

Their focus remained fixed on what had been lost in the natural, rather than on what had been declared in the spiritual.

But as followers of Christ, they were called, and so are we, to believe that what is unseen is greater than what is seen.

After appearing to three trusted followers, Jesus finally revealed Himself to the remaining eleven. Notice this: He did not come in the gentle, consoling tone one might expect. He came in authority and power, and He rebuked them for their stubborn unbelief:

Mark 16:14 (NLT) *"Still later He appeared to the eleven disciples as they were eating together. He rebuked them for their stubborn unbelief because they refused to believe those who had seen Him after He had been raised from the dead."*

And immediately after this rebuke, He gave them a command:

Mark 16:15 (NLT) *"Go into all the world and preach the Good News to everyone."*

You might wonder; Where is the compassion? Where is the comfort from the One Scripture calls the Great Comforter?

But remember:

Isaiah 55:8 (NLT) *"My thoughts are nothing like your thoughts,' says the Lord. 'And My ways are far beyond anything you could imagine."*

God is not swayed or clouded by emotion.

Where we may be overwhelmed, He remains anchored.

Where we may waver in grief, He stands in unshakable authority.

Jesus fully trusted the Father, and He calls us to do the same. He did not appear to indulge their sorrow; He came to pull them out of their emotional pit, set them back on their feet, and send them into the world with purpose and power.

Let this be a reminder for us all: Whatever we may be facing, God calls us to rise above the emotions of the moment and trust Him, even when it hurts, even when it makes no sense.

Do not let the sorrow or confusion of this passing life plant seeds of unbelief that keep you from recognizing your Risen Christ when He appears.

Light for the Path

Unbelief takes root when we let grief and circumstances overshadow God's promises, but faith rises when we fix our eyes on the unseen and trust His Word.

Deeper Light – Reflect + Respond

1. Read More

- Proverbs 1:32-33
- Psalm 112:7-8
- Isaiah 55:8–9
- Romans 3:3-4
- Hebrews 11:1

2. Journal Prompt

- Where have I allowed disappointment or sorrow to cloud my faith in God's promises?
- Have I resisted testimonies of God's power because they didn't align with my current emotions or perspective?
- What would it look like for me to rise above emotions and trust God's unshakable Word today?

3. Daily Declaration of Faith

"I walk by faith, not by sight. I believe the Word of God above my emotions, and I trust the Risen Christ."

4. Live It Out

- When emotions overwhelm you, stop and declare a promise of God out loud.
- Choose one area where doubt has lingered, and replace it with a specific Scripture of faith.
- Share a testimony of God's faithfulness with someone this week to strengthen both your faith and theirs.

Reflection

_____

_____

_____

_____

_____

_____

_____

_____

_____

_____

_____

_____

_____

_____

_____

_____

_____

_____

_____

_____

Victory over Familiarity

"Familiarity robs us of the ability to live in wonder"

Joshua Tufano

2 Corinthians 5:16 *"Therefore, from now on, we regard no one according to the flesh. Even though we have known Christ according to the flesh, yet now we know Him thus no longer."*

We've all heard about the **"spirit of familiarity"** but what exactly is it? Simply put, it's the subtle pull to view things solely through the natural realm instead of through the Spirit. This spirit often attacks our relationships.

The people in Jesus' hometown could not receive from Him because they were too *familiar* with Him in the natural. As a result, their unbelief hindered them from experiencing the miracles He carried.

Mark 6:5 NLT *"And because of their unbelief, he couldn't do any miracles among them except to place his hands on a few sick people and heal them."*

This is the spirit of familiarity at work; when we view people only according to the flesh and define them by what we see outwardly. Like yeast, if familiarity is not cast out, it can permeate every part of our spiritual walk. It shifts us from being spiritually minded to carnally minded, which only produces death:

Romans 8:6 *"For to be carnally minded is death, but to be spiritually minded is life and peace."*

We must continually look at everything through a spiritual lens, not just a natural one. All things originate in the spirit realm. When we guard our hearts in this way, we honor people no matter how familiar we are with them because we continue to see who they truly are in Christ, not just who they appear to be outwardly.

This perspective is also a powerful weapon in forgiveness. When someone wrongs us, we can look past their behavior and see who God created them to be. Perhaps in ignorance, they are acting contrary to their true identity. Seeing them through spiritual eyes empowers us to call them higher, speaking to their destiny rather than their failure.

This is exactly how God relates to us: He speaks to the finished work of who we are in Christ, not to the moments of our weakness.

Those who are easily offended often walk in familiarity because they are constantly judging others by their actions rather than by their potential in Christ. To walk in the Spirit, you must lose sight of yourself and become a servant to all, speaking prophetically into the lives of others, affirming the identity that Christ has given them.

A powerful example of this is found in the story of Gideon:

Judges 6:11-12 *"Now the Angel of the Lord came and sat under the terebinth tree which was in Ophrah, which belonged to Joash the Abiezrite, while his son Gideon threshed wheat in the winepress, in order to hide it from the Midianites. And the Angel of the Lord appeared to him, and said to him, 'The Lord is with you, you mighty man of valor!'"*

Gideon was threshing wheat in a winepress, a place where there is no wind, showing he was hiding in fear rather than acting in strength. Yet the Lord didn't call him fearful. Instead, He spoke to Gideon's true identity: **"Mighty man of valor."**

God wasn't addressing Gideon's current behavior—He was calling forth the destiny placed within him.

Behavior is merely the outward expression of what someone believes about themselves internally. God overlooks momentary actions to speak to eternal purpose. When we walk with spiritual eyes, refusing to regard anyone according to the flesh, we too can speak life-giving words that ignite destiny in others.

John 6:63 *"It is the Spirit who gives life; the flesh profits nothing. The words that I speak to you are spirit, and they are life."*

And we must not forget: we must do this for ourselves first. If this is something you struggle with, please refer to the devotion series entitled **"You Are Not Your Flesh"** and make a daily habit out of declaring those scriptures. For the way we love ourselves sets the standard for how we love others:

Mark 12:31 *"And the second, like it, is this: 'You shall love your neighbor as yourself.' There is no other commandment greater than these."*

If you find that you often judge yourself harshly or focus only on your own failures, it is likely you are doing the same to others: your children, your spouse, your friends. True love flows first from receiving how God sees you.

1 John 4:19 *"We love Him because He first loved us."*

If this resonates with you, pray this simple prayer:

Prayer of Repentance

"Father, forgive me for not seeing myself the way You see me. Today, I choose to cast down every negative word spoken over my life, and to see myself through Your eyes. Give me a revelation of Your love, so that I can walk with You and become a source of encouragement and life to others. I receive Your love today, and I thank You for it. Amen."

Light for the Path

Familiarity blinds us to God's work by keeping our eyes on the flesh, but seeing with the Spirit allows us to honor others, forgive freely, and call forth their true identity in Christ.

Deeper Light – Reflect + Respond

1. Read More

- 2 Corinthians 4:18
- Mark 6:1–6
- Romans 8:6
- Philippians 4:13
- Mark 12:31

2. Journal Prompt

- In what relationships have I allowed familiarity to blind me to God's work in others?
- Do I tend to focus on people's failures or speak into their God-given potential?
- How do I currently see myself: through the lens of my mistakes, or through the truth of who I am in Christ?

3. Daily Declaration of Faith

"I regard no one according to the flesh. I see myself and others through the eyes of Christ and speak destiny into their lives."

4. **Live It Out**

- This week, intentionally speak life-giving words over someone, affirming who they are in Christ rather than pointing out their faults.
- Write down three Scriptures about your identity in Christ and declare them daily to realign how you see yourself.
- When tempted to judge harshly, pause and ask: "How does God see this person right now?"

Reflection

_____

_____

_____

_____

_____

_____

_____

_____

_____

_____

_____

_____

_____

_____

_____

_____

_____

_____

Week 35

When Religion Hates Your Rising

John 5:8–10 *"Jesus said to him, 'Rise, take up your bed and walk.' And immediately the man was made well, took up his bed, and walked. And that day was the Sabbath. The Jews therefore said to him who was cured, 'It is the Sabbath; it is not lawful for you to carry your bed.'"*

There is a spirit that despises seeing people rise above what once bound them. Jesus often healed on the Sabbath, not by accident, but with intention, to expose the Pharisees' hypocrisy. They didn't truly care about people; they were bound to rules and regulations. Their hearts were hardened by religion, not softened by love.

The same spirit is still at work today. There will always be those who oppose your rising and use "scripture" to justify why you should stop. Consider wealthy word of faith preachers, they have sown tens of millions of dollars into the Kingdom of God, yet many Christians despise them. Why? Because their rise exposes something within them: jealousy and offense.

This is the same Pharisaical spirit disguised in devotion, but filled with envy. It hides behind religious arguments, but its true nature is revealed through criticism, slander, and self-righteous judgment. God is exposing this spirit in these last days and revealing the true remnant, those who rejoice when others rise and celebrate the power of God at work.

Think about it: it wasn't the Gentiles who handed the Messiah over to be crucified, it was the people of God. The same spirit is alive today. It is often those who claim to belong to God who persecute the ones stepping out in faith to do great exploits for the Kingdom. Why?

Because the religious spirit is perfectly fine with you practicing your faith as long as you keep quiet about it. The moment you begin to rise, walk in authority, and do mighty things for God, it provokes the modern-day Pharisees. They fear losing their platforms and being forgotten, but they mask it as a noble effort to **"protect the flock from wolves in sheep's clothing."** What they don't realize is that they've unknowingly aligned themselves with a demonic spirit, one that actively resists the earth being filled with the knowledge of God.

Habakkuk 2:14 *"For the earth will be filled with the knowledge of the glory of the Lord, as the waters cover the sea."*

And it makes perfect sense because Satan doesn't want the world to know God. He wants people lulled into complacency by religious rituals that soothe the conscience but still leave them enslaved to sin, which leads to death (**Romans 6:23**).

So don't give an ear to the Pharisaical spirit. Put on your armor. Keep pressing forward. God is raising up a people who will not be silenced.

Prepare to rise and prepare for the arrows that will come because of it. Do not be afraid. The same God who lifts you higher is the One who protects you. No arrow that flies by day will strike you (**Psalm 91:5**).

No devil can stop your rising!

No religious spirit can quench the power within you that fuels your ascent!

You were made for victory to conquer every work of the enemy through the power of Christ alive in you.

Romans 16:20 TPT *"And the God of peace will swiftly pound Satan to a pulp under your feet! And the wonderful favor of our Lord Jesus will surround you."*

So never view the enemy's challenge as your defeat. Instead, see it as the very catalyst God will use to elevate you to the next level. You were not created for collapse you were created for conquest. You were born to reign!

Everything you need for victory already dwells within you. Don't let emotions take the driver's seat. Yes, the pain may be real, but even in the midst of it, lift your hands with tears in your eyes and declare boldly:

"Thank You, God, that this pain has no power to imprison me! Thank You that I am victorious through Christ, and nothing can stop my rising! I take dominion over the spirit trying to stop me, and I declare; Out of my way! I was made for victory and I will not settle for anything less!"

Light for the Path

The spirit of religion resists your rising, but God has already empowered you to walk in victory and silence every opposing voice.

Deeper Light – Reflect + Respond

1. Read More

- John 5:8–10
- Habakkuk 2:14
- Romans 6:23
- Psalm 91:5–7
- Romans 16:20

2. Journal Prompt

- Have I ever faced resistance from others when I began to step into new levels of faith or authority?
- How can I discern between godly correction and the Pharisaical spirit that resists rising?
- Are there any people in my life right now that try to keep me down with a Pharisaical spirit?

3. Daily Declaration of Faith

"No spirit of religion can stop my rising. I walk in victory and authority through Christ within me."

4. Live It Out

- Write down an area where you sense resistance to your rising and declare God's Word of victory over it daily.
- Refuse to give place to criticism rooted in jealousy or fear; pray blessing over those who oppose you instead.
- Choose to walk in the direction God has called you, even if others oppose it. Ignore their voices and move forward with confidence!

Reflection

_____

_____

_____

_____

_____

_____

_____

_____

_____

_____

_____

_____

_____

_____

_____

_____

_____

_____

Week 36

VICTORY AND DEFEAT

Genesis 50:20 *"But as for you, you meant evil against me; but God meant it for good, in order to bring it about as it is this day, to save many people alive."*

We are not only walking in the victory of the cross; we are also walking in the reality of the enemy's defeat!

It is vital to remember that what Jesus accomplished on the cross thousands of years ago did more than give us victory over sin, death, and hell; it also disarmed and defeated the enemy of our souls.

Colossians 2:15 *"And when He disarmed the spiritual rulers and authorities, He shamed them publicly by His victory on the cross."*

Jesus stripped the enemy of his power, shamed him openly, and triumphed over him. This is the image we should hold in our hearts when we think of satan in the light of the cross. Though he may still attempt his schemes, we must remain even more mindful of his defeat and the unshakable victory we already possess in Christ.

The final weapon the enemy had against humanity was death, but Jesus took care of that once and for all.

1 Corinthians 15:55 *"O death, where is your victory? O death, where is your sting?"*

Let your words not only proclaim the victory over the enemy but also declare his ultimate defeat at Calvary.

Revelation 12:11 *"And they have defeated him by the blood of the Lamb and by their testimony. And they did not love their lives so much as to shrink from death."*

The shed blood of Jesus, combined with the testimony of His transforming work in our lives, seals the enemy's defeat for all eternity. Give your attention, your adoration, and your confession to the only One who deserves it—the One who purchased your freedom, secured your victory, and crushed the powers of darkness forever: Jesus, our Savior.

Light for the Path

The cross not only secured our victory in Christ, it sealed the enemy's eternal defeat; our testimony now declares what Jesus has already won.

Deeper Light – Reflect + Respond

1. Read More

- Genesis 50:20
- Colossians 2:15
- 1 Corinthians 15:55–57
- Revelation 12:11
- Romans 8:37–39

2. Journal Prompt

- Do I live more mindful of Christ's victory or the enemy's attacks?
- How can I let my testimony boldly declare the enemy's defeat?
- Where in my life do I need to shift from fear to faith in the finished work of the cross?

3. Daily Declaration of Faith

"Through the cross, I live in Christ's victory and declare the enemy's defeat. I am more than a conqueror."

4. **Live It Out**

- Each day this week, thank Jesus specifically for one area of victory He has already secured for you.
- Speak aloud Scriptures that declare the enemy's defeat whenever fear or doubt tries to rise.
- Declare over your life; *"I will speak not of the works of the enemy, but only of the victory I have through the blood of Jesus and the testimony of how it changed my life and made me a new creation."*

Reflection

_____

_____

_____

_____

_____

_____

_____

_____

_____

_____

_____

_____

_____

_____

_____

_____

_____

_____

NO BETTER, BUT WORSE

Mark 5:26 *"She had spent all she had and was no better, but rather grew worse."*

The testimony of the woman with the issue of blood teaches us a profound truth: when we rely solely on earthly resources, we do not just waste time, energy, and money; things can actually become worse.

Scripture tells us that even after spending everything she had on physicians, her condition did not improve. In fact, it grew worse. Why? Because the healing she needed was not in the hands of man. It was in the presence of Jesus.

Mark 5:27 (NLT) *"She had heard about Jesus, so she came up behind him through the crowd and touched his robe."*

Her faith in Jesus was the true pathway to the healing she had longed for over twelve painful years.

Mark 5:25 (NLT) *"A woman in the crowd had suffered for twelve years with constant bleeding."*

But when she finally acted in faith, something miraculous happened.

Mark 5:34 (NLT) *"And he said to her, 'Daughter, your faith has made you well. Go in peace. Your suffering is over.'"*

Faith is always present tense. Faith is **NOW**.

And now, for her, was the moment to reach for the Healer.

Did she have to spend all those years and resources to receive her healing? The answer is no.

James 5:15 (NLT) *"Such a prayer offered in faith will heal the sick, and the Lord will make you well. And if you have committed any sins, you will be forgiven."*

When we rely on God's power, authority, and truth, we can receive what we need immediately. That is exactly what happened to her.

Mark 5:29 (NLT) *"Immediately the bleeding stopped, and she could feel in her body that she had been healed of her terrible condition."*

God is not selective or partial in His blessings.

Acts 10:34 (TPT) *"Now I know for certain that God doesn't show favoritism with people but treats everyone on the same basis."*

This means we also can receive by faith what we are believing for right now.

Mark 11:22–24 (NLT) *"Then Jesus said to the disciples, 'Have faith in God. I tell you the truth, you can say to this mountain, May you be lifted up and thrown into the sea, and it will happen. But you must really believe it will happen and have no doubt in your heart. I tell you, you can pray for anything, and if you believe that you've received it, it will be yours.'"*

God's desire for His people is wholeness in every area.

3 John 1:2 (NLT) *"Dear friend, I hope all is well with you and that you are as healthy in body as you are strong in spirit."*

This includes spirit, soul, and body. Healing, provision, strength, and peace are all part of His plan.

Earthly wisdom often leads to frustration, depletion, and poor health. But godly wisdom leads to prosperity, strength, and divine health.

Proverbs 3:5–8 (NLT) *"Trust in the Lord with all your heart; do not depend on your own understanding. Seek His will in all you do, and He will show you which path to take. Don't be impressed with your own wisdom. Instead, fear the Lord and turn away from evil. Then you will have healing for your body and strength for your bones."*

It is time for the children of God to live by faith, not by what they see.

2 Corinthians 5:7 (NLT) *"For we live by believing and not by seeing."*

Jesus already paid the price, so we must stop settling for **"no better, but worse"** and start receiving everything He made available to us through His death and resurrection.

Light for the Path

Earthly resources may fail, but faith in Jesus brings immediate access to His healing, wholeness, and provision.

Deeper Light – Reflect + Respond

1. Read More

- Mark 5:25–34
- James 5:15
- Acts 10:34
- Mark 11:22–24
- Proverbs 3:5–8

2. Journal Prompt

- Where have I been relying more on human wisdom or effort than on God's power?
- What does it look like for me to reach out in faith "now" rather than waiting for conditions to improve?
- How can I begin receiving God's wholeness in spirit, soul, and body today?

3. Daily Declaration of Faith

"By faith I receive wholeness now; spirit, soul, and body. I trust in the Lord and not in my own understanding."

4. **Live It Out**

- Each morning this week, declare over your life; "Jesus is our life and the length of our days" (Deuteronomy 30:20).
- Replace one habit of self-reliance with a deliberate act of faith; pray first, trust first.
- Share your testimony of God's provision or healing with someone who needs encouragement to believe.

Reflection

_____

_____

_____

_____

_____

_____

_____

_____

_____

_____

_____

_____

_____

_____

_____

_____

_____

_____

_____

_____

_____

No Law = No Punishment

1 John 4:18 (TPT) *"Love never brings fear, for fear is always related to punishment. But love's perfection drives the fear of punishment far from our hearts. Whoever walks constantly afraid of punishment has not reached love's perfection."*

A person who does not know the heart of God will naturally lean toward trying to earn their worth through works. Often without even realizing it, we develop a habit of trying to earn God's love by our good behavior. Anyone who lives under a standard of performance also lives under the threat of punishment for falling short. When this mindset transfers into our relationship with God, we start believing that His love fluctuates based on our performance.

As a result, we may *"feel"* God's love when we're doing well and *"feel"* His displeasure when we stumble. But here's the truth: God's love already met the requirements for us through Jesus. We are no longer held to the impossible standard of the law. Hallelujah!

We can now approach God without fear of punishment because the standard has been fulfilled. It is finished! That's why the writer of Hebrews proclaimed:

Hebrews 10:1–2 *"For the law, having a shadow of the good things to come, and not the very image of the things, can never with these same sacrifices, which they offer continually year by year, make those who approach perfect. For then would they not have ceased to be offered? For the worshipers, once purified, would have had no more consciousness of sins."*

When God's wrath was poured out upon Jesus, it perfected forever all those who place their faith in Him. That means we can now approach

God without a constant, nagging sense of guilt or shame. In Christ, the stains have been washed away.

> **Isaiah 1:18** *"Come now, and let us reason together," says the Lord, "Though your sins are like scarlet, they shall be as white as snow; Though they are red like crimson, they shall be as wool."*

The law existed to continually remind people of their sin and their inability to approach God on their own. That's why sacrifices had to be made over and over. But now, only one sacrifice was needed. Christ's offering was more than enough to pay for all our sins. There is no further payment required. It has been paid in full.

Because of Jesus' sacrifice, we can now come to God as if we had never sinned. The fear of punishment no longer has a place in the life of a believer. If we are not held to a standard, then there is no punishment for failing to meet it. And that means… we are free! Forever free!

You ought to be dancing by now!

> **John 8:32** *"And you shall know the truth, and the truth shall make you free."*

> **John 8:34–36** *"Jesus answered them, 'Most assuredly, I say to you, whoever commits sin is a slave of sin. And a slave does not abide in the house forever, but a son abides forever. Therefore if the Son makes you free, you shall be free indeed.'"*

Slaves are held to a standard and are punished when they fall short. But sons? Sons are free. Christ has made us sons and daughters by paying our ransom in full.

Thank You, Jesus!

"Father, I ask You to help me to see this truth. That I would no longer see myself being held to a standard of rules and regulations, that I may be rid of the fear of punishment for not meeting those standards. I thank You for setting my heart free and empowering me to embrace Your love—the love that fulfilled the standard on my behalf and was freely given to me as a reward, as though I had kept it myself. Thank You for strengthening me to never turn back!"

Light for the Path

Because Jesus fulfilled the law, we no longer live in fear of punishment; His perfect love has set us free to live as sons and daughters.

Deeper Light – Reflect + Respond

1. Read More

- 1 John 4:18
- Hebrews 10:1–2
- Isaiah 1:18
- John 8:32–36
- Romans 8:1–2

2. Journal Prompt

- Do I ever relate to God based on performance, feeling loved when I "do well" and distant when I fail?
- How does knowing Christ fulfilled the law change the way I approach God daily?
- What would it look like to live fully free from fear of punishment?

3. Daily Declaration of Faith

"There is no condemnation for me in Christ Jesus. I am washed clean, free from fear, and I live in the love of God."

4. **Live It Out**

- Each time guilt tries to rise this week, declare Romans 8:1 out loud: *"There is therefore now no condemnation for those who are in Christ Jesus."*
- Replace self-critical thoughts with reminders of God's love and acceptance in Christ.
- Share this truth with someone who struggles with guilt or performance-based faith.

Reflection

_____

_____

_____

_____

_____

_____

_____

_____

_____

_____

_____

_____

_____

_____

_____

_____

_____

_____

_____

Freedom From Curses

"The believer who understands their authority in Christ will laugh in the face of every curse and walk in dominion."

Kenneth Hagin

Many born-again believers, unaware of the authority they've been given, become instruments in the enemy's hand when they fail to take dominion over their tongues—exposing the uncrucified flesh still at work within. Instead of releasing blessing over their brothers and sisters, they speak words laced with cursing; partnering with darkness while claiming to walk in the light.

James 3:10 *"Out of the same mouth proceed blessing and cursing. My brethren, these things ought not to be so."*

James 1:26 *"If anyone among you thinks he is religious, and does not bridle his tongue but deceives his own heart, this one's religion is useless."*

To crucify the flesh is to silence its voice. So why, even with full knowledge of the scriptures, do some believers curse their own brothers and sisters? Because it reveals unresolved jealousy, ingratitude, and discontentment within their hearts. We must learn to rejoice with those whom the Lord is using powerfully, not envy them.

The world will also hate believers who rise higher than what the world says is "allowed." But the real tragedy is when those in the church join with the world to curse God's people. Even so, have no fear the curse cannot touch you.

Exodus 12:13 ESV *"The blood shall be a sign for you, on the houses where you are. And when I see the blood, I will pass over you, and no plague will befall you to destroy you."*

Psalm 91:10 *"No evil shall befall you, nor shall any plague come near your dwelling."*

These two verses form a powerful promise: no plague, no curse, and no destruction can touch you. Why? Because the blood of Jesus, the perfect Passover Lamb, has been shed and now covers the doorposts of our spirit. We are shielded by the covenant of God, and no curse has the authority to land on us.

Proverbs 26:2 TPT *"An undeserved curse will be powerless to harm you. It may flutter over you like a bird, but it will find no place to land."* (Some Hebrew manuscripts imply the curse returns to the one who spoke it like a bird returning to its nest.)

Let that sink in: no curse can land. It may hover. It may intimidate. But it cannot fall upon you. You are divinely protected.

Psalm 64:2–4 *"Hide me from the secret plots of the wicked, from the rebellion of the workers of iniquity, who sharpen their tongue like a sword, and bend their bows to shoot their arrows bitter words, that they may shoot in secret at the blameless; suddenly they shoot at him and do not fear."*

Where does God hide us? Psalm 91:1 gives the answer:

Psalm 91:1 *"He who dwells in the secret place of the Most High shall abide under the shadow of the Almighty."*

We are hidden in Christ and no curse can reach that place. The Lord Himself has declared:

Numbers 23:20–21 NLT *"Listen, I received a command to bless; God has blessed, and I cannot reverse it! No misfortune is in His plan for Jacob; no trouble is in store for Israel. For the Lord their God is with them; He has been proclaimed their king."*

Deuteronomy 23:5 *"Nevertheless the Lord your God would not listen to Balaam, but the Lord your God turned the curse into a blessing for you, because the Lord your God loves you."*

If God has blessed you, no one, no person, no demon, can curse you. They may sharpen their tongues like swords and aim bitter words like arrows, but they cannot touch what God has covered. No unsaved person, nor any unrepentant believer operating with a Pharisaical spirit, can effectively curse you or stop your advancement. In fact, and sadly, those very curses will return upon their own heads:

Psalm 37:14–15 *"The wicked have drawn the sword and have bent their bow to cast down the poor and needy, to slay those who are of upright conduct. Their sword shall enter their own heart, and their bows shall be broken."*

God is raising His people higher and higher because we have an inheritance of blessing. Those who curse it only invite judgment upon themselves. Why would God allow a curse to fall on you when He already laid it on Christ? Even human courts don't allow someone to be tried twice after a verdict has been issued. You have already been declared not guilty.

Christ became the curse in your place so that you never would have to bear it. So, declare this over your life daily:

"I'm blessed and cannot be cursed! I'm going higher and higher, and no devil in hell can stop the forward momentum upon my life because the wind of heaven is in my sails! Thank You, Father, for it!"

Galatians 3:13–14 *"Christ has redeemed us from the curse of the law, having become a curse for us (for it is written, 'Cursed is everyone who hangs on a tree'), that the blessing of Abraham might come upon the Gentiles in Christ Jesus, that we might receive the promise of the Spirit through faith."*

Psalms 41:2 *"The Lord will preserve him and keep him alive...You will not deliver him to the will of his enemies."*

Light for the Path

Because of the blood of Jesus, no curse has power over us; every word of death is broken, and we walk in blessing and protection.

Deeper Light – Reflect + Respond

1. Read More

- James 3:10
- Proverbs 26:2
- Psalm 91:1, 10
- Numbers 23:20–21
- Galatians 3:13–14

2. Journal Prompt

- Have I ever believed that a curse or word spoken against me could limit God's blessing in my life?
- Do my words reflect blessing or cursing over myself and others?
- How can I grow in the awareness of my covenant protection in Christ?

3. Daily Declaration of Faith

"I'm blessed and cannot be cursed! I'm going higher and higher, and no devil in hell can stop the forward momentum upon my life because the wind of heaven is in my sails! Thank You, Father, for it!"

4. **Live It Out**

- Intentionally bless someone this week, especially in an area where you may have felt tempted to speak negatively.
- Write down one Scripture about God's protection and declare it over your life each morning.
- When fear of curses or opposition arises, remind yourself: Christ already bore the curse for me.

Reflection

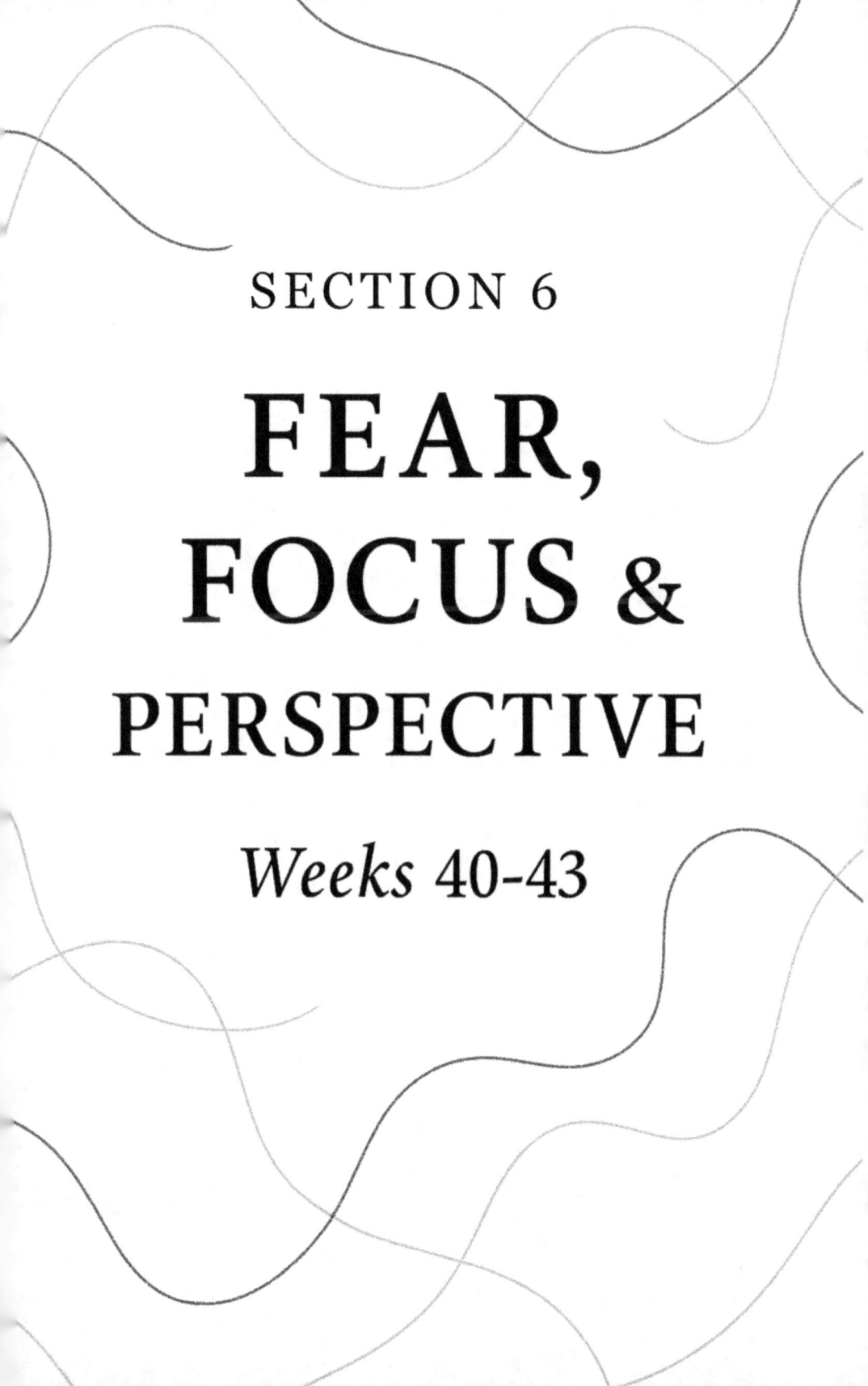

SECTION 6

FEAR, FOCUS & PERSPECTIVE

Weeks 40-43

Fearing God Over Man

Proverbs 29:25 *"The fear of man brings a snare, But whoever trusts in the Lord shall be safe."*

A snare is a trap; something that entangles and holds prey in place, with no escape unless someone else intervenes. When we choose to walk in the fear of man, we become ensnared by spiritual forces that are difficult to break free from. Fear of man leads us down paths that God never intended for us, paths where His voice is drowned out by the opinions and expectations of others.

Not only does a snare bind you, it also keeps you stuck in places you're not meant to remain. Jesus gave us clear instruction:

Matthew 10:27–28 *"Whatever I tell you in the dark, speak in the light; and what you hear in the ear, preach on the housetops. And do not fear those who kill the body but cannot kill the soul. But rather fear Him who is able to destroy both soul and body in hell."*

We are not to fear man, because man holds no authority over our soul, only God does. Man has influence only in the natural, while God reigns in both the natural and the supernatural. Therefore, when God directs our steps, we must not shrink back in fear of man's response.

Jesus said, *"What I tell you in the dark…"* but what does that mean?

Matthew 6:6 *"But you, when you pray, go into your room, and when you have shut your door, pray to your Father who is in the secret place; and your Father who sees in secret will reward you openly."*

This is the place of intimate, private communion with God; your secret place. The direction He gives you in these moments, in the **"dark"**, must be walked out boldly **"in the light."** We are not to apologize for what He has spoken, nor attempt to explain it to those who refuse to understand. Jesus said to preach what you hear, meaning, to declare it boldly without fear.

But if we're ensnared by the fear of man, this becomes difficult. We will default to following man's plans instead of God's. Yet when we fear God above all and follow His leading, no matter the cost, we position ourselves for a divine reward.

Psalm 37:5 *"Commit your way to the Lord; Trust also in Him, And He shall bring it to pass."*

He will bring it to pass openly. The blessings that come from obedience will be evident to all. The Hebrew word for **"safe"** in **Proverbs 29:25** means **"to be inaccessible, set on high."** That's powerful!

Ephesians 2:4–6 *"But God, who is rich in mercy, because of His great love with which He loved us, even when we were dead in trespasses, made us alive together with Christ (by grace you have been saved), and raised us up together, and made us sit together in the heavenly places in Christ Jesus."*

So where is Christ seated?

Ephesians 1:21 *"Far above all principality and power and might and dominion, and every name that is named, not only in this age but also in that which is to come."*

If we are seated with Christ, then we, too, are positioned far above all the power of the enemy. We are **"inaccessible high"**, untouchable by the enemy's reach, unstoppable in the will of God, and moving forward with unstoppable momentum.

This is the reward for those who trust in the Lord and follow His direction without fear of man.

If today you find yourself among those who have allowed the fear of man to guide their actions and decisions, it's time to break free from that snare!

With your heart fully engaged, pray this prayer of repentance:

Prayer of Repentance

"Father, I come before You and ask for Your forgiveness for placing greater value on the opinions of men than on Your voice. You alone bled and died for me, and You alone are worthy of my full allegiance. Strengthen me, Lord, to stand firm in the direction You have given me, even when others do not understand or agree.

Today, I choose to cast down the fear of man from my heart and instead to walk in the fear and reverence of my Father and Savior. Expose any place within me where the root of the fear of man has taken hold, and make me whole and free in those areas. I thank You for Your help, and I boldly declare, in agreement with You, that from this day forward, I am free and I will walk in that freedom!

In Jesus' name, amen."

John 8:32 *"And you shall know the truth, and the truth shall make you free."*

Light for the Path

The fear of man traps us, but trusting in the Lord lifts us high above the enemy's reach and secures us in His will.

Deeper Light – Reflect + Respond

1. Read More

- Colossians 1:13–14
- 1 John 5:18
- Psalm 37:5
- Ephesians 2:4–6
- 1 John 4:4

2. Journal Prompt

- Have I allowed fear of people's opinions to silence or delay what God has asked me to do?
- What has God spoken to me in the "secret place" that I need to boldly walk out in the light?
- How does knowing I am seated with Christ far above all powers change the way I see opposition?

3. Daily Declaration of Faith

"I fear God, not man. I trust in the Lord, and He sets me high above every snare, safe in Christ and free to walk in His will."

4. **Live It Out**

- Identify one decision where fear of man has influenced you and realign it with God's direction.
- Declare Scripture out loud whenever intimidation or pressure from others arises.
- Share one testimony of obedience to God's voice with someone who needs courage.

Reflection

_____

_____

_____

_____

_____

_____

_____

_____

_____

_____

_____

_____

_____

_____

_____

_____

_____

_____

_____

_____

FEAR: NOT THE HOLY KIND

Mark 14:54 *"But Peter followed Him at a distance."*

Why did Peter, who had followed Jesus closely and intimately for three years, suddenly choose to follow Him at a distance? Did he believe it was safer for himself to keep some space from his persecuted Messiah?

I believe Peter, like many of us, was deceived into thinking that it is safer to follow Jesus from afar. To stay comfortable. To not rock the boat. To avoid trouble and remain neutral. But the truth is: there is no safer place than being close to Jesus.

Isaiah 54:17 (MSG) *"But no weapon that can hurt you has ever been forged. Any accuser who takes you to court will be dismissed as a liar. This is what God's servants can expect. I'll see to it that everything works out for the best."*

Fear and unbelief are the very things that keep us from following Him closely; the One who desires deep, intimate relationship with us.

John 15:7 *"If you abide in Me, and My words abide in you, you will ask what you desire, and it shall be done for you."*

Intimacy cannot be developed at a distance. We must draw near.

James 4:8 *"Draw near to God and He will draw near to you. Cleanse your hands, you sinners; and purify your hearts, you double-minded."*

We were created for direct, abiding fellowship with the Father—Him in us, and us in Him.

John 17:20–23 (NLT) *"I am praying not only for these disciples but also for all who will ever believe in Me through their message. I pray that they will all be* *one, just as You and I are one—as You are in Me, Father, and I am in You. And may they be in Us so that the world will believe You sent Me... I am in them and You are in Me. May they experience such perfect unity that the world will know that You sent Me and that You love them as much as You love Me."*

Unbelief is not just a refusal to believe God's Word; it's a distrust in the One who spoke it.

And that kind of distrust is always rooted in fear.

But fear has no place in the life and identity of one who is in Christ.

2 Corinthians 5:21 *"For He made Him who knew no sin to be sin for us, that we might become the righteousness of God in Him."*

Because of Jesus, we've been given the right to confidently come before the Father. No fear. No shame. Just grace.

Hebrews 4:16 *"Let us therefore come boldly to the throne of grace, that we may obtain mercy and find grace to help in time of need."*

So we must ask ourselves:

Do we, like Peter, only follow Jesus closely when it feels *"safe"*?

Do we distance ourselves when obedience begins to cost more than we're comfortable giving?

Are we hesitant to be set apart in our families, friendships, or culture for His sake?

We must remember the promise that God gives us; the promise that whatever we willingly lose for His name's sake, we will gain back in this life multiplied! This promise should encourage us to press forward into the unknown, not to retreat into comfort."

Matthew 19:29 NLT *"And everyone who has given up houses or brothers or sisters or father or mother or children or property, for My sake, will receive a hundred times as much in return and will inherit eternal life."*

Mark 14:54 reminds us that following Jesus closely or from a distance is a daily choice. We have the freedom to decide how near we walk with Him.

Let us no longer fall for the lie that distance equals safety.

Instead, let us remember Jesus' prayer for us:

John 17:15 *"I do not pray that You should take them out of the world, but that You should keep them from the evil one."*

Following Jesus intimately brings belief, trust, boldness, and protection.

How much safer can we get?

Light for the Path

True safety is not found in following Jesus at a distance; it is found in drawing near to Him with boldness and trust.

Deeper Light – Reflect + Respond

1. Read More

- Mark 14:54
- Isaiah 54:17
- John 15:7
- James 4:8
- Hebrews 4:16

2. Journal Prompt

- Do I ever follow Jesus "at a distance" to avoid discomfort, risk, or rejection?
- What temptations of fear keep me from drawing closer to Him in full trust?
- How would my relationship with God change if I truly believed intimacy with Him is the safest place I could be?

3. Daily Declaration of Faith

"I draw near to God, and He draws near to me. I abide in Christ, I am bold in His presence, and fear has no place in my life. When I trust and believe in the perfect love of God, then fear, torment and unbelief will be cast out!"

4. Live It Out

- Take one deliberate step this week to draw nearer to God, whether through extended prayer, worship, or time in the Word.
- Speak boldly about your faith in a situation where fear might tempt you to remain silent.
- Each day, remind yourself that intimacy with God is your place of safety.

Reflection

_____

_____

_____

_____

_____

_____

_____

_____

_____

_____

_____

_____

_____

_____

_____

_____

_____

_____

Where is Your Focus?

Romans 4:19 *"And not being weak in faith, he did not consider his own body, already dead (since he was about a hundred years old), and the deadness of Sarah's womb."*

The word **"consider"** means to fix one's eyes or mind attentively upon something. Therefore, what this passage is revealing is profound: fixing your attention on the natural realm will automatically weaken your faith. When your mind is set on what you see and feel in the natural, rather than on the unseen realities of the spirit, you will live and speak according to the natural and that leads directly into weak faith. As the Word declares:

Romans 8:7-8 *"Because the carnal mind is enmity against God; for it is not subject to the law of God, nor indeed can be. So then, those who are in the flesh cannot please God."*

If you are living according to the flesh, you are not operating in faith for only faith pleases God. A carnal focus not only separates us from the power of faith, but leads inevitably to death:

Romans 8:6 *"For to be carnally minded is death, but to be spiritually minded is life and peace."*

"Death" here does not only refer to physical death, but to anything resulting from the curse: poverty, sickness, brokenness—all of which entered the world through separation from God, the Source of life. Therefore, setting your mind only on natural circumstances positions you in weakness, where the supernatural cannot easily manifest.

What, then, is the remedy? Is it to first stop walking according to the flesh, hoping that afterward you'll find yourself walking in the Spirit? No, that is the deception of the world and a trap many believers fall into, saying, *"You need to clean yourself up first, and then God can help you."* That is the furthest thing from the truth!

You don't stop walking in the flesh in order to start walking in the Spirit. You start walking in the Spirit and in doing so, you will automatically cease walking in the flesh. The Scripture is clear:

Galatians 5:16 *"I say then: Walk in the Spirit, and you shall not fulfill the lust of the flesh."*

Our only responsibility is to seek the Holy Spirit through prayer, the Word, and communion with God. As we do, we naturally and effortlessly begin to walk according to the Spirit. We are not called to **"clean ourselves up"** in our own strength, for we have no strength apart from Him. It is only through walking with the Spirit that our focus shifts from the natural to the supernatural. When that happens, our faith becomes strong, powerful, and able to move mountains.

Mark 11:22-24 *"So Jesus answered and said to them, 'Have faith in God. For assuredly, I say to you, whoever says to this mountain, "Be removed and be cast into the sea," and does not doubt in his heart, but believes that those things he says will be done, he will have whatever he says. Therefore I say to you, whatever things you ask when you pray, believe that you receive them, and you will have them.'"*

Many people claim to believe, and they may, but are they truly operating in faith? It's crucial to understand that true belief is a product of the heart, not merely of the mind. Some, through gritted teeth, declare, *"I believe! I believe!"* thinking that the act of saying it is the fullness of belief. But that is not belief, it is striving in the flesh, and it will not produce the power that faith brings.

Some might ask, *"What's the difference between belief and faith?"*

Belief can persist so long as circumstances seem favorable. But faith is revealed when you continue to stand firm on what you believe even when circumstances seem to contradict it. Faith clings to the promises of God not because of what is seen, but because of the unwavering conviction that His Word is true regardless of experience or delay.

When you do not yet see the promises of God manifest in your life, what is your response? Do you throw up your hands and say, *"I guess it's not true"*? Or do you press deeper into the Lord, contending for His promises, fully persuaded that they are true despite the present circumstances?

Those who operate in true faith are those whose attention is not fixed on the natural, but on the supernatural. They press into the Lord, knowing that if His promises are not manifesting, the fault never lies with Him but with something within themselves that must be aligned. Therefore, contend for the promises of God until they become manifest in your life. Do not lend your ears to voices of unbelief and distrust. Stand firm. Fight the good fight of faith and hold fast to every word He has spoken!

1 Timothy 6:12 *"Fight the good fight of faith, lay hold on eternal life, to which you were also called and have confessed the good confession in the presence of many witnesses."*

1 John 5:4 *"For whatever is born of God overcomes the world. And this is the victory that has overcome the world our faith."*

Light for the Path

Weak faith comes from focusing on the natural, but strong faith grows when we fix our eyes on God's Word and walk by the Spirit.

Deeper Light – Reflect + Respond

1. Read More

- Romans 4:19
- Romans 8:6–8
- Galatians 5:16
- Mark 11:22–24
- 1 John 5:4

2. Journal Prompt

- Where has my focus been more on circumstances than on God's promises?
- Am I trying to "clean myself up" before walking in the Spirit, or am I letting the Spirit do the work in me?
- How can I shift my attention daily from the natural to the supernatural?

3. Daily Declaration of Faith

> *"I walk by the Spirit and not by the flesh. My faith is strong, my focus is fixed on God's Word, and I overcome the world through Christ."*

4. Live It Out

- Catch yourself when your thoughts drift to fear or doubt, and redirect them with a Scripture promise.
- Begin each day by praying in the Spirit or declaring a verse out loud to align your focus.
- Write down one mountain in your life and speak God's Word over it daily until it moves.

Reflection

_____

_____

_____

_____

_____

_____

_____

_____

_____

_____

_____

_____

_____

_____

_____

_____

_____

_____

_____

_____

Where is Your Treasure?

Matthew 6:19-21 *"Do not lay up for yourselves treasures on earth, where moth and rust destroy and where thieves break in and steal; but lay up for yourselves treasures in heaven, where neither moth nor rust destroys and where thieves do not break in and steal. For where your treasure is, there your heart will be also."*

The main point of this scripture is the *location* of your affections. If your focus and trust are rooted in this world and its systems, your heart will naturally become attached to them. But if your focus and trust are placed in heaven, your affections will rise above earthly concerns.

This truth pairs beautifully with Paul's exhortation:

Colossians 3:1-3 *"If then you were raised with Christ, seek those things which are above, where Christ is, sitting at the right hand of God. Set your mind on things above, not on things on the earth. For you died, and your life is hidden with Christ in God."*

Paul sets this in direct contrast with what he said earlier:

Colossians 2:20 AMPC *"If then you have died with Christ to material ways of looking at things and have escaped from the world's crude and elemental notions and teachings of externalism, why do you live as if you still belong to the world?"*

The world's system enslaves people through erroneous thinking. It saturates everything around us in the natural realm, with the chief aim of keeping humanity in bondage to its limited way of thinking, preventing mankind from walking in the full potential God ordained for us.

Ultimately, it is our **"wrong thinking"** that keeps us living beneath our calling.

When we realize that we have been crucified with Christ and have died to the ways of this world, we are called to think as God thinks, even while our physical bodies remain here on earth.

We are called to renew our minds so that we think, speak, and act according to heaven's reality.

This is when heaven invades earth through us.

If we constantly keep our focus on this world and its systems, we will limit our plans based on natural restrictions (finances, health, wealth-building, etc.).

This is dangerous because when our hearts are attached to the world, we are tied to its limitations.

But when we rise to the higher calling, thinking heavenly, we walk in the supernatural.

When we plan according to the limitless potential that is inside us by the indwelling Holy Spirit, we become barrier-breakers and innovators, bringing the glory of heaven into the earth.

This high calling can only be fulfilled when we align ourselves with the Kingdom of Heaven.

That happens when we seek God above all else, and pursue His righteousness—His right way of doing things.

If we seek the heavenly, the earthly will lose its grip on our minds and hearts.

It all comes down to this:

We will walk in and experience the divine nature to the extent that we renew our minds to it.

And we renew our minds to the extent that we seek the Lord and saturate ourselves in His Word.

Thank You, Father, for Your abundant blessings!

Truly, the fear of the Lord is the beginning of wisdom and it is Your delight to give wisdom to Your children!

Light for the Path

Where we set our treasure is where our heart will follow; fixing our minds on heaven frees us from the limits of this world.

Deeper Light – Reflect + Respond

1. Read More

- Matthew 6:19–21
- Colossians 3:1–3
- Romans 12:2
- Philippians 3:20
- 2 Corinthians 4:18

2. Journal Prompt

- Where have I been storing my treasure; earthly or heavenly?
- Do my daily decisions reflect that my heart is rooted in God's Kingdom or in this world's systems?
- How can I renew my mind to align with heaven's reality?

3. Daily Declaration of Faith

"My treasure is in heaven, my heart is set on things above, and I live from the limitless power of Christ within me."

4. Live It Out

- Choose one earthly concern you've been holding onto (finances, reputation, possessions) and surrender it to God in prayer.
- Intentionally invest time this week in something eternal; encouraging someone, sharing the gospel, or serving.
- Each day, remind yourself: My true treasure is in Christ, and my heart follows Him.

Reflection

_____

_____

_____

_____

_____

_____

_____

_____

_____

_____

_____

_____

_____

_____

_____

_____

_____

_____

SECTION 7

LIVING
from
HEAVEN'S
REALITY

Weeks 44-53

COMPASSION

Colossians 3:12 MSG *"So, chosen by God for this new life of love, dress in the wardrobe God picked out for you: compassion, kindness, humility, quiet strength, discipline."*

Colossians 3:12 AMPC *"Clothe yourselves therefore, as God's own chosen ones (His own picked representatives), [who are] purified and holy and well-beloved [by God Himself, by putting on behavior marked by] tenderhearted pity and mercy, kind feeling, a lowly opinion of yourselves, gentle ways, [and] patience [which is tireless and long-suffering, and has the power to endure whatever comes, with good temper]."*

Godly compassion must return to the body of Christ. The blood of Jesus was shed to unite us as one body, not to divide us. Yet, because of a spirit of pride, many believers distance themselves from those they perceive as spiritually inferior. But this is not the heart of compassion, and it is not the heart of Jesus.

If we, the body of Christ, want to see revival and take our place in the Great Commission (**Matthew 28:18–20**), we must remember that it is the kindness of God that leads people to repentance (**Romans 2:4**).

We are not called to disregard those whose faith appears weaker than ours. We are called to reach down, support them, and help lift their faith to a higher level.

The U.S. Marines have a motto—**"Semper Fi"**—which means **"Always Faithful."** This phrase reflects more than patriotism; it represents a code of honor.

It means being loyal even when no one is watching.

It reflects a lifelong commitment.

Once a Marine, always a Marine.

This is a powerful picture of what the body of Christ is meant to be. We do not leave one another behind. As brothers and sisters in Christ, we are called to live by a spiritual code of honor, remaining loyal, present, and faithful to one another, even when no one else is watching. Just as God is always faithful to us, we are called to be faithful to one another.

The new life we have received through Jesus is meant to be marked by love, compassion, kindness, humility, strength, and discipline. We have been chosen to represent the Kingdom of God by bearing fruit that lasts. Each of us should take time to examine our lives and ask ourselves whether we are truly clothing ourselves in God's compassion. Before inspecting the fruit in others, we must first inspect our own.

John 15:16 NKJV *"You did not choose Me, but I chose you and appointed you that you should go and bear fruit, and that your fruit should remain, that whatever you ask the Father in My name He may give you."*

Light for the Path

The new life in Christ is meant to be clothed in compassion, kindness, humility, and faithfulness, reflecting God's heart to a broken world.

Deeper Light – Reflect + Respond

1. Read More

- Colossians 3:12
- Romans 2:4
- Romans 14:1, 15:1-2
- John 15:16
- Philippians 2:3–4

2. Journal Prompt

- Am I faithfully clothing myself in compassion, kindness, and humility each day?
- Do I view those with weaker faith as burdens, or as brothers and sisters to be lifted up?
- In what ways can I be "always faithful" in my relationships within the body of Christ?

3. Daily Declaration of Faith

"I am clothed in compassion, kindness, and humility. I bear lasting fruit, and I remain faithful to love and lift up the body of Christ."

4. Live It Out

- Choose one person this week who needs encouragement and intentionally speak life into them.
- Before criticizing others, pause and examine your own fruit.
- Practice humility by serving in a hidden way without seeking recognition.

Reflection

_____

_____

_____

_____

_____

_____

_____

_____

_____

_____

_____

_____

_____

_____

_____

_____

_____

_____

_____

_____

GOD IS WILLING AND ABLE

James 1:6–8 NLT *"But when you ask him, be sure that your faith is in God alone. Do not waver, for a person with divided loyalty is as unsettled as a wave of the sea that is blown and tossed by the wind. Such people should not expect to receive anything from the Lord. Their loyalty is divided between God and the world, and they are unstable in everything they do."*

Prayers of faith that are tainted with unbelief lead to instability and division. According to **James 1:7**, those whose prayers contain doubt should not expect to receive anything from the Lord. That's a strong word! James is essentially saying that if you're not praying with faith in God alone, you're wasting your time and breath.

He later explains in **James 5:16** that the prayers that do get answered are the earnest, fervent, and faith-filled prayers of a righteous person. When someone is divided in their loyalty, there is no power behind their words or requests. If you're praying to God with this kind of divided heart, there is a part of you that doubts His goodness and perfect character.

Many believers know that God can answer their prayers, but doubt creeps in around the question, *"Will He?"* The truth is, God is not only able—He is also willing.

This truth applies to every area of life, whether healing, finances, or anything in between. If He said it, He will do it. He does not make empty promises.

Numbers 23:19 MSG *"God is not man, one given to lies, and not a son of man changing his mind. Does he speak and not do what he says? Does he promise and not come through?"*

When you study the life of Jesus, you will not find a single instance where a faith-filled person came to Him and was refused healing or deliverance. Scripture says He healed them all.

Matthew 12:15 *"But when Jesus knew it, He withdrew from there. And great multitudes followed Him, and He healed them all."*

Do not let your prayers carry the stench of unbelief. Pray with the confidence, knowledge, and faith that God is not only able to answer but is fully willing. Be the one who prays fervently in righteousness and sees the results of powerful prayer. God is searching for those who will take Him at His Word. He is looking for those who will worship Him in Spirit and in truth; the truth of who He is and what He has promised to do.

John 4:23–24 NLT *"But the time is coming, indeed it's here now, when true worshipers will worship the Father in spirit and in truth. The Father is looking for those who will worship him that way. For God is Spirit, so those who worship him must worship in spirit and in truth."*

Light for the Path

Faith must rest in God's unchanging character; He is not only able to answer prayer—He is also willing.

Deeper Light – Reflect + Respond

1. Read More

- James 1:6–8
- James 5:16
- Numbers 23:19
- Matthew 12:15
- John 4:23–24

2. Journal Prompt

- Do my prayers carry full faith in God's willingness, or are they tainted with doubt?
- In what area of my life do I need to shift from hoping to trusting in His promises?
- How would my prayers change if I believed God is both willing and able every time?

3. Daily Declaration of Faith

"My faith rests in God alone. He is willing, He is able, and I will see His promises fulfilled in my life."

4. Live It Out

- Write down one specific promise from Scripture related to your current need, and pray it daily with confidence.
- When doubt rises, speak out loud: God is willing and able!
- Share a testimony of God's answered prayer with someone this week to encourage their faith.

Reflection

_____

_____

_____

_____

_____

_____

_____

_____

_____

_____

_____

_____

_____

_____

_____

_____

_____

_____

_____

_____

_____

_____

GREATER GLORY

Haggai 2:9 NLT *"The glory of this present house will be greater than the glory of the former house," says the LORD of Heaven's Armies. "And in this place I will grant prosperity," says the LORD of Heaven's Armies.*

How many times have we heard someone refer to the past as **"the good old days?"** As if their past was only filled with good times and nothing ever went wrong. Many of these people try to recreate their former lives, only to find themselves continually unsuccessful. This way of living leads to discouragement and stagnation. They become unable to live in the *present* because, unlike what the verse above says, they believe the greatest days of their lives are already behind them.

According to **Haggai 2:9**, the things that God leads us into are actually **greater than the place we are currently in.** Take a moment to let that truth settle in your heart. When we find ourselves in a season we enjoy, it is tempting to want to unpack and stay there for a while.

So when God calls us to move into something new, we may hesitate, and sometimes even disobey. This hesitation is rooted in unbelief. We struggle to believe that any other season can be as rich or meaningful as the one we are in now, or, the one we once had. But we could not be more wrong!

With every new step God calls us to take, we move from strength to strength and from glory to glory. We go from one greater season to another as we obey the Lord and follow His commands.

Psalm 84:7 *"They go from strength to strength; each one appears before God in Zion."*

2 Corinthians 3:18 *"But we all, with unveiled face, beholding as in a mirror the glory of the Lord, are being transformed into the same image from glory to glory, just as by the Spirit of the Lord."*

Do not let your past deceive you into thinking that the best has already come and gone. Trust that wherever the Lord is leading you next is greater than both your past, and your present.

Trust that He has good plans for your life, and that He will always lead you to something better and more meaningful. Believe that as His plan unfolds through your obedience, you are stepping into a future with God that is richer, deeper, and more glorious than anything you have experienced before.

Jeremiah 29:11 *"For I know the thoughts that I think toward you," says the LORD, "thoughts of peace and not of evil, to give you a future and a hope."*

Light for the Path

God never leads us backward; every step of obedience moves us into greater strength, greater glory, and a future filled with hope.

Deeper Light – Reflect + Respond

1. Read More

- Philippians 1:6
- Isaiah 43:18–19
- Proverbs 4:18
- Romans 8:28
- Ephesians 3:20

2. Journal Prompt

- Am I tempted to live in "the good old days" rather than trusting God for the future?
- Where has God asked me to move forward, but I've hesitated in unbelief?
- How would my perspective change if I believed that every new season with God is greater than the last?

3. Daily Declaration of Faith

"My path grows brighter and brighter. I move from strength to strength and from glory to glory, for my God is leading me into greater things."

4. **Live It Out**

- Identify one area where you've been reluctant to let go of the past and surrender it to God.
- Declare daily that your best days are ahead, not behind.
- Take a practical step of obedience that moves you into the "new thing" God is calling you toward.

Reflection

_____

_____

_____

_____

_____

_____

_____

_____

_____

_____

_____

_____

_____

_____

_____

_____

_____

_____

_____

_____

THE HOLY COVER UP

Genesis 9:20–27 NLT *"After the flood, Noah began to cultivate the ground, and he planted a vineyard. One day he drank some wine he had made, and he became drunk and lay naked inside his tent. Ham, the father of Canaan, saw that his father was naked and went outside and told his brothers. Then Shem and Japheth took a robe, held it over their shoulders, and backed into the tent to cover their father. As they did this, they looked the other way so they would not see him naked. When Noah woke up from his stupor, he learned what Ham, his youngest son, had done. Then he cursed Canaan, the son of Ham: "May Canaan be cursed! May he be the lowest of servants to his relatives." Then Noah said, "May the Lord, the God of Shem, be blessed, and may Canaan be his servant! May God expand the territory of Japheth! May Japheth share the prosperity of Shem, and may Canaan be his servant."*

This biblical account gives us valuable insight into how the Lord views the way we treat one another. Some may wonder what exactly Ham did wrong and why Noah would pronounce a curse on the next generation of his own son.

The answer is not only found in what Ham did, but in what he failed to do. Ham exposed his father's weakness to others rather than protecting him. Shem and Japheth, on the other hand, honored their father by covering him.

The Bible describes Noah as a righteous man, blameless in his generation, and the only person on earth at that time who walked in close fellowship with God.

Genesis 6:8–9 NLT *"But Noah found favor with the Lord. This is the account of Noah and his family. Noah was a righteous man, the only blameless person living on earth at the time, and he walked in close fellowship with God."*

Genesis 7:1 NLT *"When everything was ready, the Lord said to Noah, 'Go into the boat with all your family, for among all the people of the earth, I can see that you alone are righteous.'"*

Despite knowing his father's character, Ham saw a moment of weakness and chose to expose it. How often have we been wronged, or seen someone stumble, and decided to expose or retaliate rather than cover and restore? According to God's Word, exposing others is not how we love like Him.

Ham's poor decision brought a curse on his son Canaan. This is a sobering reminder that our choices in how we treat others have lasting consequences. Scripture tells us that the love of God covers a multitude of sins, not so people can continue sinning, but so they can receive Christ's love and have the opportunity to repent.

Romans 2:4 NLT *Don't you see how wonderfully kind, tolerant, and patient God is with you? Does this mean nothing to you? Can't you see that his kindness is intended to turn you from your sin?"*

1 Peter 4:8 NLT *"Most important of all, continue to show deep love for each other, for love covers a multitude of sins."*

Shem and Japheth chose to veil their father's sin not only from others, but also from themselves. They kept their focus on who they knew their father was, a righteous man, rather than on the mistake he made. Their choice resulted in blessing.

The love of God will always produce blessing, while the response of the flesh will always produce cursing. Do not be a Ham. Be a Shem or a Japheth.

Light for the Path

True love covers the weaknesses of others, protecting their dignity and opening the door for blessing instead of curse.

Deeper Light – Reflect + Respond

1. Read More

- Galatians 6:1–2
- Proverbs 10:12
- Matthew 7:1–2
- James 5:19–20
- Ephesians 4:2–3

2. Journal Prompt

- Do I tend to expose the weaknesses of others, or do I choose to cover and restore them?
- How have I responded in the past when I saw someone fall short?
- In what relationships is God asking me to demonstrate His covering love?

3. Daily Declaration of Faith

"I walk in love that covers, not exposes. I build others up, restore the fallen, and release blessing instead of curse."

4. Live It Out

- Resist the urge to share another person's mistake with others; instead, pray for their restoration.
- Encourage someone who is struggling by affirming their identity in Christ rather than pointing out their failure.
- Choose one relationship where you've been critical and replace criticism with intercession this week.

Reflection

_____

_____

_____

_____

_____

_____

_____

_____

_____

_____

_____

_____

_____

_____

_____

_____

_____

The Pivot into Higher Levels of Strength

2 Corinthians 12:9–10 NLT *"Each time he said, 'My grace is all you need. My power works best in weakness.' So now I am glad to boast about my weaknesses, so that the power of Christ can work through me. That's why I take pleasure in my weaknesses, and in the insults, hardships, persecutions, and troubles that I suffer for Christ. For when I am weak, then I am strong."*

Paul was facing intense religious persecution. Everywhere he went, opposition followed. He endured severe backlash and suffering for the cause of Christ. In this particular instance, he had reached a breaking point and pleaded with God to remove the burden from him. God's response, however, is striking. He essentially said, **"Paul, the reason you're struggling isn't because the persecution is too great, but because you lack the strength to endure it in your own ability. But don't worry this is exactly what My grace is for: to empower you beyond your natural limitations to fulfill the task I've given you."** As Pastor Jonathan Shuttlesworth has said, *"We have been redeemed from the curse of the law, but we have not been redeemed from persecution"* (**Mark 10:29–30**). God didn't remove the persecution from Paul's life; instead, He empowered Paul to walk through it in victory. And this is how we all grow stronger in the Spirit—by leaning into God's power and relying on His strength, not our own.

Yet, this strength can only emerge once we acknowledge our complete inability to do anything of eternal value without God's help. He is the power behind everything we do successfully for the Kingdom. Isaiah puts it this way:

Isaiah 40:29–31 *"He gives power to the weak, And to those who have no might He increases strength. Even the youths shall faint and be weary, And the young*

> *men shall utterly fall, But those who wait on the Lord Shall renew their strength; They shall mount up with wings like eagles, They shall run and not be weary, They shall walk and not faint."*

He gives power to the weak, that is, to those who admit their weakness apart from Him. This is not self-condemnation, nor is it a negative view of oneself. Rather, it's the moment of clarity when you recognize all the ways you've tried to do things for God in your own strength. This is why it may have felt like you were running into a wall over and over again. It wasn't always spiritual opposition, it was that God will not anoint your flesh to accomplish what He has called you to do by His Spirit.

We must come to the place where we abandon all our self-made plans to **"grow the ministry"** in our own strength. Planning is not wrong, but if our plans are born of the flesh, they won't produce the spiritual harvest God desires. Often, they will even lack the spiritual momentum needed to inspire others to come alongside and partner with the vision God has given. We must admit our need for the strength of the Spirit, and lay down the self-effort to fulfill God's call on our lives. That is what it means to humble yourself, recognizing how deeply and continually you need Him.

> **1 Peter 5:6–7** *"Therefore humble yourselves under the mighty hand of God, that He may exalt you in due time, casting all your care upon Him, for He cares for you."*

A proud person carries his burdens alone—a humble person lays them at the feet of Jesus.

Without God, we can do nothing. This is what Paul means when he says:

> **Romans 9:16** *"So then it is not of him who wills, nor of him who runs, but of God who shows mercy."*

Anything successfully accomplished for the Kingdom does not come from human will, discipline, or strategy, it comes from the Spirit of God, who breathes the power of heaven upon our works. We are like engines, but He is the fuel. An engine needs the combustion power of fuel to move forward; without it, it simply stands still. The same is true for us; no amount of fleshly effort can generate true spiritual power. The Spirit is our source.

He supplies the power when we humble ourselves, when we admit our need and actively seek His power over our own strength, His ability over our strategies, His ways above our intellect, and His Spirit over our self-will.

Ultimately, if the wind of heaven is not behind what you do, you will be laboring in vain.

Psalm 127:1 *"Unless the Lord builds the house, They labor in vain who build it; Unless the Lord guards the city, The watchman stays awake in vain."*

Light for the Path

God's strength is made perfect in my weakness. When I surrender, His Spirit empowers me to rise above every challenge.

Deeper Light – Reflect + Respond

1. Read More

- Zechariah 4:6
- Philippians 4:13
- John 15:5
- 2 Timothy 2:1
- Ephesians 6:10

2. Journal Prompt

- Where have I been relying on my own strength instead of God's Spirit?
- What burden do I need to lay at the feet of Jesus today?
- How has God's strength carried me in past seasons when I was at my weakest?

3. Daily Declaration of Faith

"I am strong in the Lord and in the power of His might; His Spirit empowers me to do what my flesh cannot."

4. Live It Out

- Surrender one area of life or ministry where you've been striving in your own strength, asking the Spirit to fuel it.
- Begin your prayers this week by confessing your dependence on God's strength.
- Encourage a friend who feels weary by reminding them of God's power that works best in weakness.

Reflection

THE RECIPE FOR PEACE

Philippians 4:4–7 NLT *"Always be full of joy in the Lord. I say it again, rejoice! Let everyone see that you are considerate in all you do. Remember, the Lord is coming soon. Do not worry about anything; instead, pray about everything. Tell God what you need, and thank Him for all He has done. Then you will experience God's peace, which exceeds anything we can understand. His peace will guard your hearts and minds as you live in Christ Jesus."*

According to these verses, God gives us a clear recipe for peace:

1. Always be full of joy in the Lord.
2. Rejoice in every circumstance.
3. Be considerate in all you do.
4. Live with the awareness that Jesus is coming soon.
5. Refuse to worry.
6. Pray about everything.
7. Tell God what you need.
8. Thank Him for all He has done.

When we follow this pattern, God's peace, beyond human understanding, will guard our hearts and minds in Christ Jesus.

Notice what is not included in this passage:

It does not say, ***"Figure it all out yourself."*** It does not tell us to stress, strive, or scramble to create our own plan. God never intended for us to be self-sufficient apart from Him. He wants to be our source for everything, including peace.

Peace does not come from having all the answers. As I recently mentioned on my podcast, *"Reclaiming the Night"*, we are called to rely on God, not on our own understanding or human wisdom. We might experience a temporary calm when we solve a problem our way, but the lasting peace, the peace that surpasses all understanding, comes only from Him.

When we lean on our own strength, we often find ourselves frustrated, anxious, fearful, and discouraged. That is not what God desires for us.

Consider the example of Jesus in **Matthew 14:19–21 (NLT)** *"Then he told the people to sit down on the grass. Jesus took the five loaves and two fish, looked up toward heaven, and blessed them. Then, breaking the loaves into pieces, he gave the bread to the disciples, who distributed it to the people. They all ate as much as they wanted, and afterward, the disciples picked up twelve baskets of leftovers. About 5,000 men were fed that day, in addition to all the women and children!"*

Jesus was faced with what seemed like lack, yet He did not panic or rush to create a plan. He **looked up** to heaven, **blessed** what He had, and **trusted** the Father. His gratitude for what seemed insufficient brought miraculous multiplication.

This principle still applies to us: thankfulness opens the door to abundance. When we place what we have in God's hands, He blesses and multiplies it. Human effort might produce temporary results, but God's provision brings abundance along with peace.

Because what good is abundance if we have no peace to enjoy it?

Philippians 4:19 NKJV *"And my God shall supply all your need according to His riches in glory by Christ Jesus."*

Let God be your source today. Trust Him. Thank Him. Pray. And watch His peace fill your heart as His provision meets your every need.

Light for the Path

Lasting peace is not found in solving every problem but in trusting God, thanking Him, and letting His presence guard my heart and mind.

Deeper Light – Reflect + Respond

1. Read More

- Isaiah 26:3
- John 14:27
- Colossians 3:15
- Psalm 55:22
- 2 Thessalonians 3:16

2. Journal Prompt

- Which step of Paul's "recipe for peace" is most difficult for me to practice right now?
- How has gratitude shifted my perspective in past seasons of difficulty?
- What would it look like to let God's peace guard my mind today?

3. Daily Declaration of Faith

"The peace of God rules my heart and mind; I refuse worry, I choose prayer and thanksgiving, and I live secure in Christ."

4. **Live It Out**

- Write down three specific things you are thankful for today and present them to God in prayer.
- When worry arises this week, immediately turn it into prayer instead of internal dialogue.
- Share encouragement with someone who is anxious, reminding them of God's promise of peace.

Reflection

MYSTERIES REVEALED

Ephesians 3:3 *"As I briefly wrote earlier, God himself revealed his mysterious plan to me."*

Matthew 13:11 *"He answered and said to them, 'Because it has been given to you to know the mysteries of the kingdom of heaven, but to them it has not been given.'"*

God delights in revealing His mysterious plans to His people. Jesus affirmed this when He told Peter that it was not human wisdom that revealed His identity, but the Father Himself.

Matthew 16:16–17 *"Simon Peter answered, "You are the Messiah, the Son of the living God." Jesus replied, "You are blessed, Simon son of John, because my Father in heaven has revealed this to you. You did not learn this from any human being."*

Earthly wisdom can never lead us deeper into the knowledge of God; it cannot unveil the hidden truths woven throughout Scripture. This is why some can sit under the same powerful teaching yet walk away unaffected, while others, hearing the very same message, leave stirred with fresh revelation, awakened by the Holy Spirit.

Paul and Peter are clear examples of men who had ears to hear what the Spirit of God was saying, and they benefited greatly because of it. Consider Peter: Jesus specifically told him in which fish a shekel would be found—a silver coin used to pay the temple tax—so that they could honor their civil duties without offense.

Matthew 17:27 *"However, we don't want to offend them, so go down to the lake and throw in a line. Open the mouth of the first fish you catch, and you will find a large silver coin. Take it and pay the tax for both of us."*

These examples emphasize why it is essential to seek the Lord for ourselves rather than relying on man alone. It is not man's role to reveal the mysteries of God to us; his role is to confirm what the Spirit of God has already spoken to our hearts.

Jesus repeatedly declared, *"He who has ears to hear, let him hear"* (see **Matthew 11:15; 13:9; 13:43**). He is looking for those who will listen with their hearts and receive the supernatural truths He is imparting. He seeks those who will worship the Father in spirit and in truth.

John 4:24 *"For God is Spirit, so those who worship him must worship in spirit and in truth."*

These are the ones who walk by faith and continue to grow in the knowledge of God's Word. These are the ones who uncover the deep mysteries of the unseen God. May we be counted among them.

Light for the Path

God reveals His mysteries to those who seek Him with open hearts, not relying on human wisdom but listening for His Spirit.

Deeper Light – Reflect + Respond

1. Read More

- Daniel 2:22
- 1 Corinthians 2:9–10
- Proverbs 25:2
- Colossians 1:26–27
- Jeremiah 33:3

2. Journal Prompt

- When has God revealed something to me in a way that human wisdom never could?
- Am I seeking God's voice directly, or relying too heavily on others to hear Him for me?
- What mystery of His Word or His plan am I asking Him to unfold in my life right now?

3. Daily Declaration of Faith

"Holy Spirit, I believe that You alone reveal the deep mysteries of the Unseen to me, and that man is used to confirm it."

4. Live It Out

- Spend 10 minutes in quiet prayer, asking God to reveal something fresh from His Word.
- As you read Scripture today, pause and invite the Holy Spirit to make one verse come alive.
- Write down one "mystery moment" this week where you sensed God revealed something to you.

Reflection

_____

_____

_____

_____

_____

_____

_____

_____

_____

_____

_____

_____

_____

_____

_____

_____

_____

_____

_____

FAITH TURNS WEAKNESS INTO STRENGTH

Hebrews 11:33–34 NLT *"By faith these people overthrew kingdoms, ruled with justice, and received what God had promised them. They shut the mouths of lions, quenched the flames of fire, and escaped death by the edge of the sword. Their weakness was turned to strength. They became strong in battle and put whole armies to flight."*

By faith, the men and women in Scripture transformed their weaknesses into strength. The supernatural victories they experienced were made possible only through their unwavering trust in God. That same faith is available to us today. Though they were weak in the natural, their confidence in the spiritual made them strong.

Faith is described as *"the reality of what we hope for; the evidence of things we cannot see"* (**Hebrews 11:1**). As we cling to the promises of God, faith grows in our hearts and gives birth to strength, empowering us to walk in the good works He prepared for us long ago.

Ephesians 2:10 NLT *"For we are God's masterpiece. He has created us anew in Christ Jesus, so we can do the good things He planned for us long ago."*

Faith does not deny our present symptoms or difficult circumstances; instead, it boldly declares that **God's Word is greater**. A person of faith who consistently speaks the truth of Scripture over their life becomes strong, immovable, and fruitful. They will begin to see tangible results.

James 5:16 NLT *"…The earnest prayer of a righteous person has great power and produces wonderful results."*

You can recognize a person of faith by their joy; even in hardship. Their countenance reflects peace because their eyes are fixed not on the **seen**, but on the **unseen**. Their hope is anchored in heaven, not swayed by the storms of earth. They believe God has a purpose for their life and will not allow circumstances or voices of doubt to stop them.

According to Scripture, it is the faithful, those without wavering or unbelief, who receive the promises of God.

James 1:6–8 NLT *"But when you ask him, be sure that your faith is in God alone. Do not waver, for a person with divided loyalty is as unsettled as a wave of the sea that is blown and tossed by the wind. Such people should not expect to receive anything from the Lord. Their loyalty is divided between God and the world, and they are unstable in everything they do."*

You will either be filled with faith or filled with the world. That decision carries both present and future consequences. But those who trust in what is unseen will find their weakness turned to strength and will inherit every promise God has spoken over their lives.

Light for the Path

Faith does not erase weakness; it transforms it into strength, anchoring us in God's unshakable promises.

Deeper Light – Reflect + Respond

1. Read More

- Isaiah 40:29–31
- 2 Corinthians 12:9–10
- Romans 4:20–21
- 1 Peter 1:6–7
- 1 John 5:4

2. Journal Prompt

- Where do I feel weak right now, and how can I invite faith to strengthen me in that place?
- Am I declaring God's Word over my life with consistency and conviction?
- What promise has God spoken that I need to hold onto without wavering?

3. Daily Declaration of Faith

"By faith, my weakness is turned to strength. I am strong in the Lord and walk in His promises with unshakable confidence."

4. Live It Out

- Identify one area of weakness and write down a Scripture promise that speaks strength into it.
- Each morning this week, declare that verse over your life with faith.
- Share a testimony of God's strength in your weakness with someone who needs encouragement.

Reflection

_____

_____

_____

_____

_____

_____

_____

_____

_____

_____

_____

_____

_____

_____

_____

_____

_____

_____

_____

GIVE CREDIT WHERE CREDIT IS DUE

James 1:13–15 NLT *"And remember, when you are being tempted, do not say, 'God is tempting me.' God is never tempted to do wrong, and he never tempts anyone else. Temptation comes from our own desires, which entice us and drag us away. These desires give birth to sinful actions. And when sin is allowed to grow, it gives birth to death."*

Stop trying to give God the credit for the temptations you face. According to the Bible, temptation comes from your flesh and from Satan. It is rooted in your own desires, which try to lead you away from Him. These flesh-driven desires lead only to death. God is good and always leads you in the way of life and life abundant. **Can I get an amen!**

John 10:10 *"The thief does not come except to steal, and to kill, and to destroy. I have come that they may have life, and that they may have it more abundantly."*

Only good and perfect things come from God, and that truth never changes. Your flesh will always try to pull you toward death, but God consistently leads you toward life. So the next time you're tempted to give in to those fleshly desires, make sure you give credit where it is due. It's not God tempting you, it's your flesh!

James 1:16–17 NLT *"So don't be misled, my dear brothers and sisters. Whatever is good and perfect is a gift coming down to us from God our Father, who created all the lights in the heavens. He never changes or casts a shifting shadow."*

The Word of God says that those who belong to Christ have already crucified the flesh along with its sinful desires.

Galatians 5:24 *"And those who are Christ's have crucified the flesh with its passions and desires."*

So if you belong to Him, then those desires that lead to death have already been put to death. Just like Jesus, your example, you fight the enemy and your flesh with the truth of God's Word.

Jeremiah 23:29 NLT *"Does not my word burn like fire?" says the Lord. "Is it not like a mighty hammer that smashes a rock to pieces?"*

The Word of God is a powerful tool in the hands of His children. It is like a mighty hammer that smashes fleshly desires to pieces. God gave you His Word to use it as a sword against the temptations of your flesh and the attacks of the enemy. If you are not walking in **overwhelming victory**, perhaps you are not using your sword the way it was meant to be used.

Proverbs 18:20-21 NLT *"The right words bring satisfaction. The tongue can bring death or life; those who love to talk will reap the consequences."*

When the battle comes knocking at your door, use the sword of the Spirit to remind your enemies that the desires leading to death have already been crucified in your life. You have been made new in Christ.

Light for the Path

God never tempts us; temptation comes from the flesh and the enemy, but His Word equips us with victory.

Deeper Light – Reflect + Respond

1. Read More

- 1 Corinthians 10:13
- Matthew 26:41
- Romans 6:11–14
- Ephesians 6:10–11
- Hebrews 4:15–16

2. Journal Prompt

- Have I ever blamed God for something that was really the pull of my flesh?
- What desires do I need to confront and crucify so they no longer drag me toward death?
- How can I use God's Word more effectively as a sword when temptation comes?

3. Daily Declaration of Faith

"I have crucified the flesh with its desires, and I walk in victory through the power of God's Word."

4. **Live It Out**

- When temptation comes this week, speak a Scripture out loud instead of trying to fight it silently.
- Memorize one verse that will serve as your "sword" in moments of weakness.
- When you overcome a temptation, thank God immediately and give Him glory for your victory.

Reflection

_____

_____

_____

_____

_____

_____

_____

_____

_____

_____

_____

_____

_____

_____

_____

_____

_____

_____

_____

The Power of the Seed: Be a Sower!

Luke 8:5 *"A sower went out to sow his seed…"*

A seed contains life. Within it is the power to reproduce, but only after its own kind. An apple seed will never produce an orange tree; a seed can only bring forth what it was created to carry. This was set in place by God as a spiritual law from the very beginning:

Genesis 1:11 *"Then God said, 'Let the earth bring forth grass, the herb that yields seed, and the fruit tree that yields fruit according to its kind, whose seed is in itself, on the earth'; and it was so."*

Without seed there is no life, but seed alone is not enough. It carries potential, yet it must be placed in soil in order to grow. A seed was made for soil, and without it, it cannot fulfill its purpose. That is why the condition of the soil—our hearts—is so important. Soil will either create an atmosphere of limitation or open the door to limitless possibility. This is why the parable of the sower is so vital: it is a blueprint for transforming the soil of our hearts so the seed of God's Word can take root and flourish (see the devotion **"Healing Is in Your Spirit: For Your Heart"** for a deeper dive).

Too often people fix their eyes on the harvest without giving thought to the seed. Imagine a farmer standing in an empty field, saying, *"I want corn to grow here,"* but never planting a single kernel. We would call him foolish, because we know that without planting, there can be no reaping. In the same way, if we want to see a specific harvest in our lives, we must first sow the right seed. Many are disappointed with the harvest they receive, not realizing it is simply a harvest of what they have been sowing. Some want life while speaking death, prosperity while practicing poverty, or health while sowing words of sickness and defeat.

Everything we do is a seed; from where we give our money, to how we spend our time, to the very words we allow to leave our mouths.

Proverbs 18:20–21 declares, *"A man's stomach shall be satisfied from the fruit of his mouth; from the produce of his lips he shall be filled. Death and life are in the power of the tongue, and those who love it will eat its fruit."*

If we desire to see God's promises come to pass, we must speak His Word rather than what the natural world, or, our flesh tells us. The Bible warns us:

Romans 8:6 *"For to be carnally minded is death, but to be spiritually minded is life and peace."*

All seeds contain life, but life is released only when the seed is planted and surrendered. God promises that the principle of seedtime and harvest will remain as long as the earth endures:

Genesis 8:22 *"While the earth remains, seedtime and harvest, cold and heat, winter and summer, and day and night shall not cease."*

When we grasp this truth, we begin to live differently. Instead of hoarding, we give freely. Instead of speaking what we feel, we speak what God has spoken. Instead of withholding our service, we serve generously. Understanding the power of the seed frees us to prosper in every area of life, not through striving, but through aligning with God's design.

This is the backbone of the Kingdom of God because it perfectly fulfills His law, spoken in this scripture:

Matthew 7:12 *"Therefore, whatever you want men to do to you, do also to them, for this is the Law and the Prophets."*

When we realize that everything we sow eventually returns to us, we learn to treat others as we ourselves want to be treated. This is the very definition of walking in God's love—choosing to be others-focused instead of self-focused.

Philippians 2:4 reminds us, *"Let each of you look out not only for his own interests, but also for the interests of others."*

When we understand both the love of God and the power of our seeds, we sow with intentionality, knowing the harvest will not only bless us but also overflow to others. Imagine if everyone lived with this mindset; concerned not only with their own needs but also with the needs of those around them. This is how the family of God was meant to function. But it begins with you, recognizing the power of the seed God has placed in your hands, and sowing it toward the harvest you desire.

Light for the Path

Every harvest begins with a seed. What you sow with your words, time, and actions will grow into the life you live tomorrow.

Deeper Light – Reflect + Respond

1. Read More

- Galatians 6:7–9
- Hosea 10:12
- 2 Corinthians 9:6–8
- James 3:18
- Isaiah 55:10–11

2. Journal Prompt

- What kind of harvest am I currently seeing in my life?
- Are there areas where I've been sowing negative seeds through words, actions, or attitudes?
- What specific seeds can I begin sowing today that will align with the harvest I want to see?

3. Daily Declaration of Faith

"I sow the Word of God into every area of my life, and I believe it will produce a harvest of life, blessing, and abundance."

4. Live It Out

- Take time today to evaluate the words, actions, and habits you've been sowing. Are they aligned with the harvest you desire?
- Speak Scripture over your life, give generously, and choose to invest in others with the expectation of a Kingdom harvest.
- Protect your heart from bitterness, doubt, or fear; keep it tender and ready to receive God's Word so the seed can take root and grow.

Reflection

_____

_____

_____

_____

_____

_____

_____

_____

_____

_____

_____

_____

_____

_____

_____

_____

_____

_____

The Earth's Witness

A gasp resounds through my pillars and halls,

For I could see the One sent from above to call,

Those back from the depths of death and grief,

Though they trampled me down and laid me beneath.

Beneath their calling and commission,

Casting aside glory, receiving extradition.

Yet now I see this gross injustice; the answer I can never quarry.

That they would take the One and crucify the Lord of glory.

I weep and lament, knowing just penalty is imminent,

Yet amazed, for I knew not the One's intent.

For two days I wallow in darkness, unsure how to recover.

Such evil! To ask for a thief and murderer instead of the true Lover.

My tear-stained eyes look upon the grave and stone.

"The cold lips of the grave's mouth never to open," I groan.

Yet something miraculous leaves me breathless,

The stone cracks in two, revealing the new garment He's dressed in.

Glory indeed! For death cannot overcome Life.

Forever ended is the strife!

Yet more glorious still is what next occurs;

The same ones who betrayed Him may now be transferred.

From death to life and tears to joy.

For without measure is the gift given to destroy,

The works of wickedness, now made clean,

By grace now covered and serene.

"How could such love exist?" I cry out.

Desiring punishment, for I doubt;

Such wrongs could be overlooked by a single act.

"Justice is served with precision and tact.

I always knew what against Me would transpire,

Yet nothing can quench the love of My Fire.

It burns, not seeking sin's remuneration,

But longing to redeem the offspring of My creation.

Now it is complete, wrought by My Son's hands.

The ones with scars that will forever stand.

Signs that though the greatest treason was committed,

My love can't be stopped; through it, you are acquitted."

Now I rejoice, knowing soon His sons will be revealed,

And the glory bestowed will no longer be concealed.

Therefore I wait in anticipation,

Longing for the day all will be one nation.

Not considering from where you hail,

But in the One family that will never fail.

Thus the greatest injustice has been paid,

By the King, though to the cross He went dismayed.

Yet He did not consider its shame or pain,

Only that it would wash away sin's stain.

Now stand, you people, in the truth.

Living forever in the Savior's youth.

For all has been forgotten,

And through His Life you are now son's begotten.

—*Joshua Tufano*

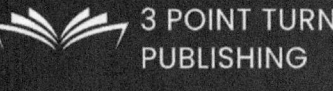

3 POINT TURN Ministries

FOLLOW US ON
All Podcast Platforms

Instagram
@3.pointturn
@mireya.tufano
@tufanovich

Facebook
@3.pointturn
@mireya.tufano
@tufanovich

YouTube
@3PointTurnMinistries

TUNE IN WEEKLY FOR UPLIFTING CONTENT!

www.ingramcontent.com/pod-product-compliance
Lightning Source LLC
Chambersburg PA
CBHW060410130626
46555CB00005B/2024